Dear Jane

Happy Christmas '93

Richard ~ Annie
with love x

A
Little Light
Weeding

My vines are going on gloriously, white bunches hang like water-spouts and black ones like thunder-clouds. Anyone looking at my vines would say, 'This is your role my good fellow, stick to it; any ass can write novels (at least in the opinion of the publishers); but to make a vine needs intellect.'

R D BLACKMORE

Also by Richard Briers
and published by Robson Books

Coward and Company
English Country Churches

A
LITTLE LIGHT
WEEDING

Richard Briers

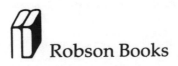
Robson Books

First published in Great Britain in 1993 by Robson Books Ltd, Bolsover House, 5–6 Clipstone Street, London W1P 7EB

Copyright © 1993 Complete Editions
The right of Complete Editions to be identified as author of this work has been asserted by them in accordance with the Copyright, Designs and Patents Act 1988

Designed by HAROLD KING

British Library Cataloguing in Publication Data
A catalogue record for this title is available from the British Library

ISBN 0 86051 883 3

Set in Bembo by Columns Production and Design Services Ltd, Reading.
Printed in Great Britain by Butler & Tanner Ltd, Frome and London.

DEDICATION

To my mother Morna and my sister Jane who, on inheriting a garden consisting mainly of concrete, transformed it into a colourful, romantic spot yet spent hardly a penny; to Peter Kane, without whose help in my garden my back would have gone long ago; and to my wife, Annie, who rushes out of the house at intervals to stop me cutting everything down to ground level, this little book is dedicated.

CONTENTS

PREFACE

The actor's life is one of insecurities and uncertainties. When we are 'resting' we are convinced we shall never be offered another job. When we are acting in the theatre we quickly become restless repeating the same part night after night. The longed for West End success quickly becomes a chore when the excitement and terrors of the first night have worn off. Even the buccaneering spirit of a long provincial tour or taking a production to a foreign country can be eroded by constant travelling and living out of a suitcase.

It is not surprising therefore that many generations of actors, from Ellen Terry to Laurence Olivier, have found a sense of continuity, security and solace in the gentler and less transitory art of creating a garden.

Mark you it's not true of all actors. For every actor besotted with his garden I could name you another who wouldn't stray from the big city and who regards the country as 'a million miles from Central Casting'.

One such was Sir Henry Irving, the great Victorian actor, who formed a legendary partnership with Ellen Terry at the Lyceum Theatre. Seated one day in Miss Terry's beautiful garden he gave it a cursory glance and remarked, 'Not at all bad – make a good set for *As You Like It*!'

I didn't develop a *real* interest in gardening myself until my forties, at about the same time as the television series *The Good Life* cast me as a suburban convert to self sufficiency who found that the answer to the meaning of life lies in the soil.

However, it was my Grandad who first told me to get behind a mower and push, when I was about ten years old. I didn't enjoy it at all and never did. I suspect my late conversion to gardening was the result of investing in a petrol mower that required no pushing at all. In fact it was so powerful it occasionally took me along with it.

Grandad was a secret pruner. Not many plants were allowed to get over eight inches high in his garden. I inherited this passion for pruning away at things and the family can always tell where I am in the garden by the sound of manic clipping.

My father, normally a rather highly strung chap, was only really happy when digging his vegetable patch. My mother and Jane, my sister, were always absolutely brilliant at growing things from seeds and cuttings. Jane maintains that cuttings are an excellent weapon against the cutbacks of a recession. The important thing is to ask before you cut of course, or gardening friends will regard you as a pest on a par with greenfly.

I regret my late conversion to the joys of gardening because to be a really knowledgeable gardener I will need to live to 150! However, I enjoy the losing battle with nature in my own amateur way, learning more and more as I go along. I also count myself lucky that I have lived in the same house, in a comparatively countrified area of London, for over 20 years. During that time my wife Annie and I have been able to watch our garden grow and develop, we have learned by our mistakes and rejoiced in our successes and created a haven away from the hustle and bustle of showbiz.

As I have become more absorbed in my garden I have also come to relish reading about gardens and gardening. There is so much good stuff written on this endlessly fascinating topic that it has not been easy to select only a few short extracts from the great classic and standard gardening works. Francis Bacon, Alexander Pope, Miss Mitford, Joseph Addison, Gertrude Jekyll, Vita Sackville-West – what a pleasure it is to read what they have to say and respond to it as freshly as if you were talking with them today.

It is also rewarding to be able to include the work of some of the great writers that I have been introduced to as a result of my chosen profession. Not only Shakespeare, with his instinctive genius for everything that motivates human nature and who quite rightly pointed out (in *Henry VI*) that Adam was the first gardener. But also poets such as Wordsworth, Marvell, Keats and Southey. I make no apology for including some of the best known poems in the language. They have deserved their fame because they say so much about gardens and nature in a way that gets straight to the heart of the matter. I believe we should positively choose to reconsider them at frequent intervals and try to find fresh insights in them. Every actor knows the challenge of trying to make well-known words sound fresh and new. What would happen if actors opted not to tackle Hamlet's famous soliloquies simply because they have been heard so often before?

Dipping into the delightful gardening reminiscences of the likes of Beverley Nichols or Cecil Beaton, I feel rather like one of those people who buys every cookery book ever published but never cooks a recipe. I could never contemplate the daunting task of creating a garden on the scale that they did; but how I enjoy sharing the satisfaction, the sorrows, the smells, sounds and colours of their successes so brilliantly brought to life in their writing.

At the same time it is so important not to be intimidated by the great gardening achievers. To my mind a garden is a happier place if you can keep competitiveness outside the garden gate. A fulfilling garden is one which suits your way of life and gives contentment. If you lead a busy life, as most of us do, don't be too ambitious or guilt – the curse of the gardening classes – will raise its ugly head and that elusive sense of contentment will disappear. Not too many flower beds, a few well chosen trees and shrubs, an efficient, well serviced lawnmower, a sharp pair of shears, and your garden will look fine yet still leave you time to sit down, enjoy your handiwork and leaf through these pages while you get to grips with 'a little light weeding'.

Richard Briers

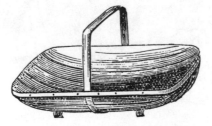

ADVICE

This is a tricky one for a self-confessed late convert to gardening. I have a good few years' experience under my belt by now but in gardening terms, where Capability Brown and his ilk might plant a tree with a view to what it might look like in two hundred years, I am a mere babe in arms.

My advice to you is to listen to what *other* people have said and written. Favourite gardening gurus of mine include the late, and very great, Fred Streeter. This stalwart of the BBC's radio gardening programmes was pure joy to listen to. He had nearly ninety years of gardening experience to share with his listeners yet he condensed it into simple, straightforward advice that always made total sense.

Here's one of Fred's fundamental rules which I have found by experience to be absolutely bang on the nail.

> Here's a tip for any gardener. Decide on a little plot of land you're going to work on this morning or this afternoon. Size it up carefully so you're sure you can cope with it – and then don't dare touch anything else until that first job is finished.

This, and many other words of wisdom can be found in the excellent book by Fred's radio colleague, Frank Henning, entitled *Cheerio Frank, Cheerio Everybody* which was how he always signed off his programmes.

At the other end of the advice scale comes H J Byron. This prolific Victorian actor and dramatist wrote over 150 plays, including many of the most popular pantomimes. His speciality was puns, most of them rather dreadful. I suspect he knew more about comic timing than tilling the soil but that didn't prevent him from coming up with a pun on the subject of gardening.

> The gardener's rule applies to youth and age:
> When young 'sow wild oats', but when old, grow sage.

The old jokes are always the best!

APPLES

One or two well placed trees give a garden style. Maybe it's the memory of all those hard-up days as a young actor but I like my trees to be useful and not merely decorative. One of the big pleasures of our garden is a Bramley apple which produces the loveliest pink blossom in the spring time and outsize cooking apples in the autumn.

Some years we are really well organized. We pick the apples as soon as they are ripe, eat the most perfect baked with brown sugar, cinnamon and mixed fruit and topped with thickly whipped cream, and make the rest into purée for the freezer. This means we can make crumbles and pies for several months' worth of Sunday lunches. People seem quite amazed to be eating delicious home produce from a *London* garden and I enjoy the reputation of a true son of the soil.

In other years things don't go quite according to plan. The blossom comes out on cue, and the apples arrive without prompting but Annie and I are rather remiss in gathering in our little harvest. The lovely fruit begins to fall to the ground and gets attacked by wasps. We pull ourselves together and move on to Plan B – Penny Keith's delicious Apple Chutney.

Penny Keith, is a gifted actress who has also been blessed with many other talents including being a marvellous gardener and cook. In *The Good Life* she played my snobbish neighbour Margot and she and Paul Eddington, who played her husband, have become our firm friends. Her recipe for chutney is designed to use up windfalls so it has become a staple of the Briers household. It's so simple even I can make it.

APPLE CHUTNEY

4lbs windfall apples, cored and chopped   1 pint vinegar
1lb roughly chopped onions   1 tsp ground ginger
1 clove crushed garlic   1 tsp salt
1lb sultanas   ½ tsp black pepper
1lb soft brown sugar

Place all the ingredients in a very large saucepan. Bring to the boil and simmer gently for *about* four hours until thick and brown. Stir occasionally with a wooden spoon to prevent it catching the base of the saucepan. Pot while still hot. Delicious with wholemeal bread and strong cheddar cheese.

Of course we shall never know if the redoubtable Mrs Beeton had the makings of an actress, but she was certainly the Superwoman of the nineteenth century. What that woman didn't know about matters domestic really wasn't worth knowing. All that amazing knowledge was distilled into her classic book *Mrs Beeton's Book of Household Management*.

Annie is lucky enough to have found a very battered and well used copy which may be one of the first editions. It is *so* well used, by, I like to imagine, a wholesome farmer's wife with ample, bread-kneeding forearms and rosy cheeks, that the front few pages are missing so we can't be sure. Anyway Mrs Beeton turns out to be a mine of information on the humble apple.

THE APPLE

This useful fruit is mentioned in Holy Writ; and Homer describes it as valuable in his time. It was brought from the East by the Romans, who held it in the highest estimation. Indeed, some of the citizens of the 'Eternal city' distinguished certain favourite apples by their names. Thus the Manlians were called after Manlius, the Claudians after Claudius, and the Appians after Appius. Others were designated after the country whence they were brought; as the Sidonians, the Epirotes, and the Greeks. The best varieties are natives of Asia, and have, by grafting them upon others, been introduced into Europe. The crab, found in our hedges, is the only variety indigenous to Britain; therefore, for the introduction of other kinds we are, no doubt, indebted to the Romans. In the time of the Saxon heptarchy, both Devon and Somerset were distinguished as *the apple country*; and there are still existing in Herefordshire some trees said to have been planted in the time of William the Conqueror. From that time to this, the varieties of this precious fruit have gone on increasing, and are now said to number upwards of 1,500. It is peculiar to the temperate zone, being found neither in Lapland, nor within the tropics. The best baking apples for early use are the Colvilles; the best for autumn are the rennets and pearmains; and the best for winter and spring are russets. The best table, or eating apples, are the Margarets for early use; the Kentish codlin and summer pearmain for summer; and for autumn, winter, or spring, the Dowton, golden and other pippins, as the ribstone, with small russets. As a food, the apple cannot be considered to rank high, as more than the half of it consists of water, and the rest of its properties are not the most nourishing. It is, however, a useful adjunct to other kinds of food, and, when cooked, is esteemed as slightly laxative.

MRS BEETON
1861

APPLES

Behold the apples' rounded worlds:
juice-green of July rain,
the black polestar of flowers, the rind
mapped with its crimson stain.

The russet, crab and cottage red
burn to the sun's hot brass,
then drop like sweat from every branch
and bubble in the grass.

They lie as wanton as they fall,
and where they fall and break,
the stallion clamps his crunching jaws,
the starling stabs his beak.

In each plump gourd the cidery bite
of boys' teeth tears the skin;
the waltzing wasp consumes his share,
the bent worm enters in.

I, with as easy hunger, take
entire my season's dole;
welcome the ripe, the sweet, the sour,
the hollow and the whole.

LAURIE LEE

Here's to thee, old apple-tree;
Hence thou mayst bud, and whence thou mayst blow,
And whence thou mayst apples bear enow!
Hats full! caps full!
Bushel, bushel sacks full!
And my pockets full, too! Huzza!

ANON

AUTUMN

I find that the physical hard work of an autumn garden – tidying, sweeping, planting ready for the next growing season, and doing what I can in the way of mulching and staking to make sure everything survives the winter – is the ideal therapy for being stuck in a stuffy rehearsal room all day. It also takes my mind off all the worries and anxieties which beset an actor preparing for a new role. An hour's hard digging is a good way of getting the artistic ego back in the right perspective!

In my selection for autumn I have included the ode *To Autumn* by Keats. At first I feared it might seem too much of a cliché but then I thought, 'How many people know anything more than the first couplet? Not many I bet.' So I have followed my own preference and kept it in. To my mind it is one of the most beautiful poems ever written. It communicates instantly with the reader without any unnecessary fuss and yet it says so much more than just the sum total of the words.

To round off this group I've chosen all the pleasures of a good autumn dinner with a poem guaranteed to make your mouth water. A man needs his reward after all that virtuous digging and sweeping.

But to begin with, another nugget of down to earth advice from that fount of gardening wisdom, Fred Streeter:

> Let's look at that little business of sweeping up the leaves in Autumn. . . . First thing to do, once you've got your broom or your besom out of the shed, is to see which way the wind is blowing. . . . Then be sure to sweep *with* the wind. You'd be surprised how many gardeners forget that simple tip and as soon as they get to the end of the garden and think the job's nearly done, all the leaves have blown back to where the poor chap started.

Fred Streeter

TO AUTUMN

I

Season of mists and mellow fruitfulness,
   Close bosom friend of the maturing sun,
Conspiring with him how to load and bless
   With fruit the vines that round the thatch-eves run:
To bend with apples the mossed cottage-trees,
   And fill all fruit with ripeness to the core;
   To swell the gourd, and plump the hazel shells
   With a sweet kernel; to set budding more,
And still more, later flowers for the bees,
Until they think warm days will never cease,
   For summer has o'er-brimmed their clammy cells.

II

Who hath not seen thee oft amid thy store?
   Sometimes whoever seeks abroad may find
Thee sitting careless on a granary floor,
   Thy hair soft-lifted by the winnowing wind;
Or on a half-reaped furrow sound asleep,
   Drowsed with the fume of poppies, while thy hook
   Spares the next swath and all its twinèd flowers;
And sometimes like a gleaner thou dost keep
Steady thy laden head across a brook;
Or by a cyder-press, with patient look,
Thou watchest the last oozings hours by hours.

III

Where are the songs of spring? Aye, where are they?
   Think not of them, thou hast thy music too —
While barrèd clouds bloom the soft-dying day,
   And touch the stubble-plains with rosy hue.
Then in a wailful choir the small gnats mourn
   Among the river sallows, borne aloft
   Or sinking as the light wind lives or dies;
And full-grown lambs loud bleat from hilly bourn;
   Hedge-crickets sing; and now with treble soft
   The red-breast whistles from a garden-croft;
   And gathering swallows twitter in the skies.

JOHN KEATS

Close and slow, summer is ending in Hampshire,
   Ebbing away down ramps of shaven lawn where close-
     clipped yew
Insulates the lives of retired generals and admirals
   And the spyglasses hung in the hall and the prayer-books
     ready in the pew
And August going out to the tin trumpets of nasturtiums
   And the sunflowers' Salvation Army blare of brass
And the spinster sitting in a deck-chair picking up stitches
   Not raising her eyes to the noise of the 'planes that pass
Northward from Lee-on-Solent. Macrocarpa and cypress
   And roses on a rustic trellis and mulberry trees
And bacon and eggs in a silver dish for breakfast
   And all the inherited assets of bodily ease
And all the inherited worries, rheumatism and taxes,
   And whether Stella will marry and what to do with Dick
And the branch of the family that lost their money in Hatry
   And the passing of the *Morning Post* and of life's climacteric
And the growth of vulgarity, cars that pass the gate-lodge
   And crowds undressing on the beach
And the hiking cockney lovers with thoughts directed
   Neither to God nor Nation but each to each.
But the home is still a sanctum under the pelmets,
   All quiet on the Family Front,
Farmyard noises across the fields at evening
   While the trucks of the Southern Railway dawdle . . . shunt
Into poppy sidings for the night —

Louis MacNeice

NOVEMBER

The mellow year is hasting to its close;
The little birds have almost sung their last,
Their small notes twitter in the dreary blast —
That shrill-piped harbinger of early snows:
The patient beauty of the scentless rose,
Oft with the morn's hoar crystal quaintly glassed,
Hangs, a pale mourner for the summer past,
And makes a little summer where it grows:
In the chill sunbeam of the faint brief day
The dusky waters shudder as they shine,
The russet leaves obstruct the straggling way
Of oozy brooks, which no deep banks define,
And the gaunt woods, in ragged, scant array,
Wrap their old limbs with sombre ivy twine.

HARTLEY COLERIDGE

UNDER THE AUTUMN GARDEN

It would soon be time for ploughing again. Already the gangster gulls were gathering daily in the rotting stubble that had lain there since Charlie cut his wheat and spread muck, back in September.

November began tomorrow and Matthew, leaning on the twilight wall, recalled that with November came Sir Oliver, when he might be seen again on the footpath. Sir Oliver, if he had ever lived, had died in the fevery fogs of a medieval autumn, and in the season of his death he could yet be seen, stomping, as only a knight in full armour could stomp, down the slope from Pallingham church, and up to Myhill Street.

Sir Oliver must surely be the most boring ghost in the county. Other Broadland villages boasted flaming monks, headless horsemen, phantom coaches, and, excessively, an entire Roman legion. Pallingham had only Sir Oliver, trudging glumly up and down the footpath like any law-abiding citizen.

Matthew knew of no one who had ever seen him, which rendered him even more boring.

JAN MARK

AN AUTUMN DINNER

Four fresh-opened oysters,
Soft as grey velvet,
Cold as – deep-sea water;
One long-stemmed glass
Half full of light Rhinewine,
Tasting of fruit-flowers.

Soup from late peas,
Mint, their faint flavour,
With it a mouthful
Of lightest East India.

Sole, bubbling and brown,
Showing soft white to the fork,
Bone-patterned, roe-inlaid.
Wise, reticent Meursault.

Slices of saddle
And tiny potatoes,
Cooked soft and succulent.
Beaune, Grêves Enfant-Jésus.

A plump basted woodcock,
Well done, yet undone,
Cold celery salad
And then – the great Chambertin.

Here, chilled mountain strawberries
Straight from the Vosges,
Kirsch-flavoured cream,
And a glass of Tokay.

Bear in the Stilton
Ripe in its turban!
Now serve Oporto,
Not too light, not too heavy.

End in aromas –
Delicate cognac,
Scent of fine coffee,
Blue smoke of Havanas.

Wit, kindness, peace,
Shared between humans
Rise from this culture
Of two glorious senses,
Spurned by the arid
And narrow-soul'd pundit.

TREVOR BLAKEMORE

BATS

Bats have had an undeserved bad press, probably because they are so closely associated with the vampire legend. They seem rather delightful little chaps to me, and I love to see them sweeping round the garden at night, silently hoovering up all the insects which plague us.

If I can digress for a moment or two on the subject of vampires it really is amazing where that word seems to crop up. In the theatre the trap doors in the stage from which the demon king and assorted baddies appear is called a vampire trap. And whenever I see Noël Coward's brilliant play, *Hay Fever*, I'm amused to be reminded that the word vamp is short for vampire — the sort of woman who eats you alive!

I love Noël Coward's plays and I adored Noël Coward. He really was as witty as his reputation, which is quite a feat. I remember once in rehearsal one of the actors struggling to get his tongue around a sentence in French and failing every time. Eventually Coward, who hated it when the cast was not word perfect for the first rehearsal, asked rather testily 'Do you speak French?' The unfortunate actor attempted a nonchalant reply in French, '*Un petit peu*,' to which Noël responded icily 'I never think that's really quite enough, do you?'

For me he summed up the attitude of theatre people to what they do when he said, 'The only way to enjoy life is to work. Work is much more fun than fun.' From what I know of people who garden for a living, or who create great gardens, they share the same attitude. Gardening, like acting, is not a job, it's a way of life.

But to return to the subject of bats. I have chosen this charming extract from Gilbert White's *Natural History and Antiquities of Selborne*. Even before I became a keen gardener I was fascinated by the wider subject of natural history and for many years I have collected copies of old books on the subject. Gilbert White's book is one of the great classics on this subject and this piece about a tame bat is a delightfully observed moment.

I was much entertained last summer with a tame bat, which would take flies out of a person's hand. If you gave it anything to eat, it brought its wings round before the mouth, hovering and hiding its head in the manner of birds of prey when they feed. The adroitness it showed in shearing off the wings of the flies, which were always rejected, was worthy of observation and pleased me much. Insects seemed to be most acceptable, though it did not refuse raw flesh when offered; so that the notion that bats go down chimneys and gnaw men's bacon seems no improbable story. When I amused myself with this wonderful quadruped, I saw it several times confute the vulgar notion, that bats, when down on a flat surface, cannot get on the wing again, by rising with great ease from the floor. It ran, I observed, with more despatch than I was aware of; but in a most ridiculous and grotesque manner.

GILBERT WHITE

BEES

I am a great admirer of bees. I love to see them buzzing around the garden being busy, particularly when I have my feet up after a good Sunday lunch. I firmly believe in work. As Jerome K Jerome so wisely said, I am such a believer in work I could sit and look at it for hours, and the same goes for bees. I have deliberately planted a variety of blue flowers, including lavender and buddleia, in order to encourage the little fellows. It is reassuring to the environmentalist in me to reflect that not far from the suburban fringes of London there must be swarms in hives, or even wild bees, who are filling their honeycombs with nectar from my garden.

However, I have not enjoyed many close encounters with the bee population and their keepers, being content to admire from a distance. That is, until recently. I had offered to clear the rubbish from my aunt's old garden shed. Having finally reached floor level I was pulling out a rather nasty piece of rotting carpet when an angry buzzing sound began. To my horror a swarm of bees, about the diameter of a large dinner plate and clearly in a state of high irritability, was beginning to rise from the ground.

I haven't moved so rapidly since I was in Ray Cooney's fast-moving farce, *Run For Your Wife*. In fact I had exited from the shed before you could *say* Cooney.

I retreated into Aunty's bungalow and, having reassured her (though not myself) that I had the matter completely under control, I telephoned the council. They informed me that they could do nothing, as bees are a protected species, and gave me the phone number of a 'Bee Man' with the delightful name of Sycamore.

I rang him at once.

'It's Richard Briers here,' I said.

'You're having me on,' he said.

'No, no, it's *really* me,' I yelled, 'and I've just been threatened by several hundred squatter bees in my aunt's shed.'

'I don't believe it,' he said, 'I've been practising *The Good Life* myself for years – I've got hens, goats, bees . . .'

'Lovely,' I interrupted hastily, 'would you like a few hundred more?'

'All my hives are full, but as it's you I'll be over a bit later when they're drowsy,' he replied, and rang off.

Early that evening Aunty and I, huddled behind the reassuring double glazing, watched him manoeuvre the bees (which were of the Bumble variety) with infinite skill and care into a box. He took them off and deposited them in a nearby wood, thus earning our eternal gratitude. Great men these 'Bee Men'.

THE BEE-KEEEPER

I can see old Gregory attending to the bee-hives with the calm, gentle movements which characterize all experienced bee-keepers. He invariably talked to the bees when he was attending them, and one day when, as a small child, I was watching him I asked 'Do the bees understand what you are saying to them, Gregory?' 'Understand, Missie?' he replied. 'Just as much as horses and dogs and cattle; it stands to sense an' reason they do! An' sometimes I thinks they understan' more nor we do.'

ELEANOUR ROHDE *Herbs and Herb Gardening*
1936

What two extraordinary substances to be made, by little creatures, out of roses and lilies! What singular and lively energy in nature to impel these little creatures thus to fetch out the sweet and elegant properties of the coloured fragrances of the garden, and serve them up to us for food and light – honey to eat, and waxen tapers to eat it by!

LEIGH HUNT

I will not account her among the very good House-wives, that wanteth either Bees or skilfulness about them.

WILLIAM LAWSON
1618

KEEPING BEES

A swarm should always be put into a *new* hive, and the sticks should be *new* that are put into the hive for the bees to work on; for, if the hive be old, it is not so *wholesome*, and a thousand to one but it contain the embryos of *moths* and other insects injurious to bees. Over the hive itself there should be a cap of thatch, made also of clean rye-straw; and it should not only be *new* when first put on the hive; but, a new one should be made to supply the place of the former one every three or four months; for, when the straw begins to get rotten, as it soon does, insects breed in it, its smell is bad, and its effect on the bees is dangerous.

The hives should be placed on a bench, the legs of which mice and rats cannot creep up. Tin round the legs is best. But, even this will not keep down *ants*, which are mortal enemies of bees. To keep these away, if you find them infest the hive, take a green stick and twist it round in the shape of a ring, to lay on the ground, round the leg of the bench, and at a few inches from it; and cover this stick with *tar*. This will keep away the ants. If the ants come from one home, you may easily *trace them to it*; and when you have found it, pour *boiling water* on it in the night, when all the family are at home. This is the only effectual way of destroying ants, which are frequently so troublesome. It would be cruel to cause this destruction, if it were not necessary to do it, in order to preserve the honey, and, indeed, the bees too.

WILLIAM COBBETT *Cottage Economy*
1823

BEE

Thou art a miser, thou busy, busy Bee!
  Late and early at employ;
Still on thy golden stores intent,
Thy summer in heaping and hoarding is spent,
  What thy winter will never enjoy;
Wise lesson this for me, thou busy, busy Bee!

Little dost thou think, thou busy, busy Bee!
  What is the end of thy toil.
When the latest flowers of the ivy are gone,
And all thy work for the year is done,
  Thy master comes for the spoil.
Woe then for thee, thou busy, busy Bee!

ROBERT SOUTHEY

31

BIRDS

Birds, like bees, are an essential part of a garden. I really love it when spring comes around and the birds start singing early in the morning. That's when you know winter is really over. For some years now I have had two robins in my garden. Knowledgeable friends said this was not possible because robins are too territorial. Clearly these two have accepted arbitration on the subject and have agreed to divide the territory down the middle because I never catch them having undignified scraps over who owns what.

One bird I have no desire to share *my* territory with is the local heron, for reasons why *see* Water on page 233. Yet I have to admit he looks rather magnificent flapping idly above the lawn with his over-long legs drifting behind him like a feathered daddy longlegs. I never cease to be amazed at the amount and variety of wildlife which flourishes in London just a hop, skip or wing flap from the M4 and the Hammersmith roundabout. We have entertained hedgehogs and urban foxes in our own small patch.

It is a pleasure to the Eare to heare the sweet notes and tunes of singing Birds, whose company a man shall be sure to have in an Orchard.

RALPH AUSTEN *A Treatise of Fruit-Trees*
1653

As my Garden invites into it all the Birds of the Country, by offering them the Conveniency of Springs and Shades, Solitude and Shelter, I do not suffer any one to destroy their Nests in the Spring, or drive them from their usual Haunts in Fruit-time. I value my Garden more for them being full of Blackbirds than Cherries, and very frankly give them Fruit for their Songs. By this Means I have always the Musick of the Season in its Perfection, and am highly delighted to see the Jay or the Thrush hopping about my Walks, and shooting before my Eye across the several little Glades and Alleys that I pass through.

JOSEPH ADDISON *The Spectator*
1712

The blackbird amid happy trees
The lark above the hill,
Let loose their carols when they please,
Are quiet when they will.

WILLIAM WORDSWORTH

'CLASS' IN THE GARDEN

Theatre is really the ultimate classless society. I love the tolerance which theatre folk have. It might not be quite the oldest profession on offer for women but it was certainly one of the first to treat women as equals. There's a terrific camaraderie among actors and the only thing that matters is how good you are at what you do. In some ways it's better to be thought of as 'an actor's actor', which implies the respect of your peers, than to be a star of stage and screen. It's true the profession has its great figures but this has nothing to do with what they wear or who they know and everything to do with the outstanding quality of their work.

Odd then to think that gardening, which is a passion for people from all sides of the social spectrum, and where you might assume that the quality of what you create is all that matters, still allows the question of class to creep in. If you lacked confidence in your own judgement and cared what people thought then it used to be a safe bet to keep everything white (apart from the leaves that is). This would indicate clearly that you were not a sucker for bright, vulgar bedding plants and appreciated the subtlety of Vita Sackville-West's impeccable white garden at Sissinghurst. Now even this piece of advice can be dangerous. If you keep everything white you lose face because it is quite clear you lack confidence in your own judgement and care what people think. What a social minefield it all is!

Personally I don't really care for gnomes. Not because I think they lack ton but because most of them look too manically happy, which, for some obscure reason, depresses me. However, I make it a point of honour to have a couple of gnomes in my garden as a silent testimony to the right of gnome-lovers everywhere to do their own thing without fear of snide remarks.

One of these peers out, with his huge gnomic grin, from a window in my garden shed and usually raises an answering laugh from visitors. The second is a very irritable looking concrete gnome pushing a wheelbarrow from here to eternity. I quite like him. He reminds me of me!

To begin the section on the vexed question of 'class' in the garden I have chosen this hilarious and slightly worrying piece by Jilly Cooper. I wonder if her friend knew that the Queen Mother grows Peace in *her* garden?

The Englishman traditionally loves his garden. It needs cherishing and tending, but doesn't answer back. It is hardly surprising, therefore, that class distinction should be almost more rampant outside the house than in it. Once again garden centres — like furniture shops — do a roaring trade because of snobbery. People are constantly ripping up the plants and paving stones of previous owners — 'Too ghastly, my dear'. I remember being mystified once when a friend came to stay. We were having tea outside, enjoying the sunshine and the quiet (for once the aeroplanes were silent) when suddenly she fixed me with a beady eye and said,

'You know, it's frightfully common to have Peace in one's garden.'

It was a few minutes before I realized that she was referring to the beautiful pink and yellow rose next to the magnolia which flowers so gallantly and continually all summer. I can only suppose that she thought it was vulgar because it is so universally popular.

In the same way Caroline Stow-Crat wouldn't touch gladioli, begonias and chrysanthemums, or fuchsias — except in the conservatory. Also on the index would be gaudy bedding plants like petunias, French marigolds, calceolarias, cinerarias, calendulas, salvia, Californian poppies, zinnias, asters and yellow daisies, although Michaelmas daisies and white daisies are all right. Colour is also important: the white and green tobacco plants are much more upper-class than the red or mauve ones and dark red wallflowers better than yellow or mauve. Trails of pale blue lobelia are all right, but Oxford blue is very common, particularly when combined in military rows with white alyssum and scarlet geraniums. Caroline wouldn't be keen on any flower of a different colour to that which nature intended — blue roses, brown irises, pink forget-me-nots or daffodils. Daffodils, she feels, should be planted in long grass, not in flower beds. She hates tulips. If she had rhododendrons she would have not individual ones, but great clumps lining the drive. A friend once asked a West Country peer how he achieved his magnificent multi-coloured display.

'Oh, I move them around,' said the peer. 'When I want to change the colour scheme, I just get twenty men up from the factory.'

'Yellow and green should never be seen', so Caroline would soon rip out anything variegated such as laurels or, even worse, privet and mother-in-law's tongue.

Some trees are more upper-class than others: one thinks of the great flat-bottomed oaks, beeches, limes and chestnuts, that look, as Taine said, as though they'd been tended for hundreds of years like the children of rich parents.

If you discount the cedars planted by Capability Brown, indigenous trees are considered much smarter than foreign ones, which is why the white double cherry scores over the imported pink one, and why the Stow-Crats tend to despise the silver birches and conifers of Surrey. Willow trees are all right growing naturally by a lake or stream, but would be considered the height of vulgarity in the middle of a suburban lawn, particularly if planted in a circle of earth.

The suburbs in spring, with their candy-floss mass of pink and white cherry, dark pink crab-apple, almond, laburnum and lilac, are quite beyond the pale. Pink hawthorn, although considered much more common by the upper classes than white, is for some reason more acceptable in the suburbs.

JILLY COOPER, *Class*

THE SOCIAL ACCEPTABILITY OF CALCEOLARIAS

It was in my fourth year at Merry Hall that Oldfield suddenly threw us all into alarm and despondency by announcing that he was not going to pay his annual visit to the Chelsea Flower Show.

I shall never forget the occasion. It was a warm day in the middle of May, and Gaskin told me the news just after dinner.

'But that's out of the question,' I exclaimed. 'He's always gone. He and Mrs Oldfield. They look forward to it all through the year.'

'He says he's got too much to do.'

'But if I got the odd man to come an extra day a week . . . two extra days?'

'He says it still wouldn't make any difference.'

I finished my dinner in a mood of some despondency. If Oldfield did not go to the Flower Show I had a suspicion that I should never hear the last of it. It had been his custom to go up early on the morning of the third day, returning at about nine o'clock; and he usually hovered around on the lawn, in his black Sunday suit, before going to bed, in order to catch me and exchange notes. One year it was the vegetable display of the Farmers Union that caught his fancy, another year he would dilate on the rival claims of the principal seedsmen. And always he connected the glories of the present with the glories of the past, attaching to some particular flower the characteristics of one of his past employers. Thus, concerning calceolarias and the late Mr and Mrs Dove, for whom he had worked before the days of Mr Stebbing. . . .

'They was the most beautiful calceolaries I ever did see, today . . . twice the size of when I grew 'em, and all sorts of shades they never had before. Now Doovz couldn't abide calceolarias. At least, they *could* abide 'em in the beginning, but Mrs Doove, she began to get ideas when Mr Doove made his money. And one day she read in t'paper that calceolarias weren't smart no more, and nobody liked 'em in society. That was in 1910, that was. And Mrs Doove was all for society. So she come to me and say "Oldfield, chuck 'em away, the whole God's collection of 'em." So I asks her why. And she says nobody likes calceolarias no more. So I says to her as I liked 'em. "That may be," she said, "but the best people don't like 'em." So I says to her, "What you mean is they're not *oop* enough for you."'

BEVERLEY NICHOLS *The Gift of a Home*

38

Planes was a horrible house. It was an overgrown cottage, that is to say, the rooms were large, with all the disadvantages of a cottage, low ceilings, small windows with diamond panes, uneven floorboards, and a great deal of naked knotted wood. It was furnished neither in good nor in bad taste, but simply with no attempt at taste at all, and was not even very comfortable. The garden which lay around it would be a lady water-colourist's heaven, herbaceous borders, rockeries, and water-gardens were carried to a perfection of vulgarity, and flaunted a riot of huge and hideous flowers, each individual bloom appearing twice as large, three times as brilliant as it ought to have been and if possible of a different colour from that which nature intended. It would be hard to say whether it was more frightful, more like glorious Technicolor, in spring, in summer, or in autumn. Only in the depth of winter, covered by the kindly snow, did it melt into the landscape and become tolerable.

NANCY MITFORD *The Pursuit of Love*
1947

In truth, nothing can be more vulgar than my taste in flowers, for which I have a passion. I like scarcely any but the common ones. First and best I love violets, and primroses, and cowslips, and wood anemones, and the whole train of field flowers; then roses of every kind and colour, especially the great cabbage rose; then the blossoms of the lilac and laburnum, the horse-chestnut, the asters, the jasmine, and the honeysuckle; and to close the list, lilies of the valley, sweet peas, and the red pinks which are found in cottagers' gardens. This is my confession of faith.

MARY RUSSELL MITFORD to WILLIAM ELFORD
17 April 1812

Harold to Vita   Teheran

31 December 1926

Darling, I don't like rhododendrons — I am sorry. I don't mind them in a big place round a big lake. But I think they are as out of place at our cottage as a billiard-table would be. To me it is exactly the same. Then I don't like putting in big things (as distinct from small flowers) which are not indigenous: I am opposed to specimen trees. You see, I think our stunt at Long Barn is to keep the Kentish farm background, and on that background to embroider as much as we like. But rhododendrons would spoil the background. I feel sure you agree really — only you think, 'He doesn't understand that the pond garden has to be backed and enclosed by something large and bushy and dark.' But I do understand this, and I agree that if rhododendrons were natives to Kent they would be exactly and absolutely what we want. But they are *not* natives and we should spoil our lovely Kentish atmosphere. I'm sure I am right. But what then can we have? Well, cob nuts, and hazel, banked right at the back, with holly as a background to them — and in front some syringa and flowering shrubs. Yes, I know it's difficult. Shrubbery is a great problem if one is to avoid the suburban. But it's not a problem which can be solved by rosie-dendrons. I don't mind holly so long as it's not variegated. But be clever and think of all the indigenous things and get an idea of derivatives. What about more flowering peaches against a background of holly? I think that the pond garden wants a great deal of dark background. In fact I think the nuttery should be made with a plantation of dark trees. One wants the pond to look like a clearing in a wood: not like a piece of water in a rock garden.

Vita and Harold: The Letters of Harold Nicolson and
Vita Sackville-West
1910–62

RHODODENDRONS

John Betjeman once described them to me as a 'stockbrokers' flower'. If this is indeed the case, the stockbrokers are to be felicitated.

BEVERLEY NICHOLS *Garden Open Today*
1963

Now let us hear a little on behalf of that much maligned fellow the suburban gardener. Generations of readers have enjoyed reading the exploits of the great hero of suburbia, Pooter, his devoted wife and helpmeet, Carrie, and their friends, Cummings and Gowing, in *Diary of a Nobody*. Their daily problems and little triumphs and their dogged insistence that 'people are happier who live a simple, unsophisticated life' were brilliantly brought to life on the stage by Judi Dench and her husband Michael Williams. I was gratified to discover this extract in which Pooter approaches gardening in his customary spirit of optimism and good humour.

April 14. Spent the whole of the afternoon in the garden, having this morning picked up at a bookstall for fivepence a capital little book, in good condition, on *Gardening*. I procured and sowed some half-hardy annuals in what I fancy will be a warm, sunny border. I thought of a joke, and called out Carrie. Carrie came out rather testy, I thought. I said: 'I have just discovered I have got a lodging-house.' She replied: 'How do you mean?' I said: '*Look at the boarders*.' Carrie said: 'Is that all that you wanted me for?' I said: 'Any other time you would have laughed at my little pleasantry.' Carrie said: 'Certainly – *at any other time*, but not when I am busy in the house.'

GEORGE and WEEDON GROSSMITH *Diary of a Nobody*
1892

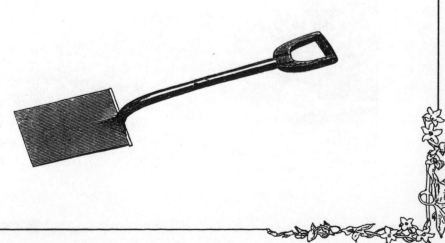

Some years before Pooter flourished in the terraces of Victorian north London, Charles Dickens had already noted and identified the same gardening species and described him, and his good lady, of course, in *Sketches by Boz*.

There is another and a very different class of men, whose recreation is their garden. An individual of this class, resides some short distance from town – say in the Hampstead-road, or the Kilburn-road, or any other road where the houses are small and neat, and have little slips of back garden. He and his wife . . . have occupied the same house ever since he retired from business twenty years ago . . .

In fine weather the old gentleman is almost constantly in the garden; and when it is too wet to go into it, he will look out of the window at it, by the hour together. He has always something to do there, and you will see him digging, and sweeping, and cutting, and planting, with manifest delight. In spring-time there is no end to the sowing of seeds, and sticking little bits of wood over them, with labels, which look like epitaphs to their memory; and in the evening, when the sun has gone down, the perseverance with which he lugs a great watering-pot about is perfectly astonishing . . . The old lady is very fond of flowers, as the hyacinth-glasses in the parlour-window, and geranium-pots in the little front court, testify. She takes great pride in the garden too: and when one of the four fruit-trees produces rather a larger gooseberry than usual, it is carefully preserved under a wine-glass on the side-board, for the edification of visitors, who are duly informed that Mr So-and-so planted the tree which produced it, with his own hands.

CHARLES DICKENS *Sketches by Boz*
1836

This 'fabe' sketch from the radio programme *Round the Horne* is a brilliant parody of those terrible designers who make you feel that everything in your house and garden lacks style and fashion. I adored Kenneth Williams's performance as Sandy and thought it was brilliantly complemented by Hugh Paddick as Julian. Their outrageous performances were beautifully contrasted with Kenneth Horne's determined ordinariness. May I suggest that you find a couple of friends and read this sketch aloud, recreating Jule's and Sand's nasal campness and Kenneth Horne's reassuringly bluff tones and playing up the *double entendres* for all their worth. Fantabulosa!

FABE HOMES AND BONA GARDENS

Sandy   Hello Mr Horne, ducky. It's us – Jule and Sand.

Horne   Look, you'd better come in before the neighbours see you. Now, this is my living-room.

Sandy   Ugh! Nasty!

Horne   What's wrong with it?

Sandy   Well, it's a bit vintage years of Hollywood, isn't it. I couldn't live in a place like this, could you, Jule?

Julian	Oooh no – I couldn't be doing with that flocked wallpaper – that'll have to go for a start. Gives me the horrors, it does. Oooh – ugh – I shall have to go and have a lie down.
Sandy	Now look what you've done to him. You might have had the place redecorated before you called us round here. See, when he sees wallpaper like that it completely clogs up his self-expression. Never mind, Jule, you can express yourself on his drapes.
Julian	Yes, we've got some bona curtain materials.
Sandy	Yes, fabe! Show him your swatch.
Julian	Yes – now, you have your plum velvet, you have your hessian, you have your silk –
Horne	Wild?
Sandy	Absolutely insane!
Julian	Then you have your various florals – your rhododendrons entwined with forget-me-nots, your creeping ivy, then you have your dandelion. Take your pick.
Horne	No, I wouldn't pick a dandelion; you know what they say. No – I fancy something a little different.
Julian	Well, it's all down to black leather then.
Horne	Black leather curtains?
Julian	Very kinky.
Sandy	And if they wear, you can always have them half-soled and heeled.
Sandy	Yes – put him down for leather curtains. 'Course, it means all that tat furniture'll have to go. It's quite out of keeping. What do you fancy, Jule?
Julian	I see Danish teak everywhere.
Sandy	Fabe!
Julian	A touch of Victoriana – say a chaise longue or a what-not. Do you fancy a what-not in the corner, Sand?
Sandy	Well, you want me to be frank, don't you? I mean, you like me to be blunt. You know me – tell the truth and shame the devil – well, frankly, man to man, I'm not besotted with the idea. It doesn't sing.
Horne	Well, that's a relief anyway. I don't think I could have stood a singing what-not.

Julian	Wait a minute, wait a minute. It's coming to me, it's coming to me. I've got it, I've got it – Palais de Versailles – gilt caryatids, full-length mirrors, chandeliers.
Sandy	Oh fantabulosa! Yes, but I think that ceiling'll have to go – it won't fit in.
Julian	Yes, and that wall'll have to go – that don't fit in, neither.
Sandy	Let's face it, Jule – everything'll have to go – I mean, none of it fits in. Right, that's settled then. Now let's have a vada at this garden of yours.
Horne	It's through here. . . .

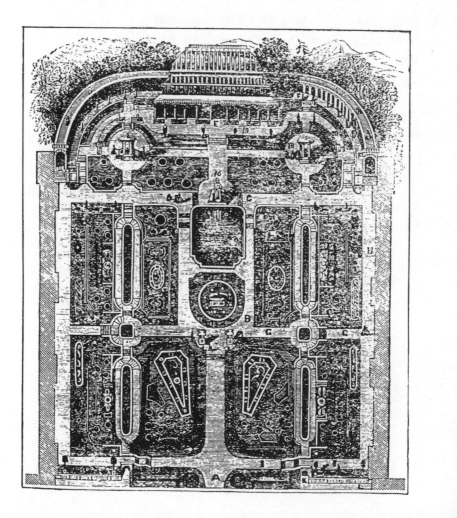

Sandy	Ugh! Nasty! I couldn't be doing with a garden like this, could you, Jule? I mean, all them horrible little naph gnomes – ooh – ugh!
Julian	Oh no – it's a bit Noddy in Toyland, ennit? All that grass – that'll have to go – I mean, *grass* in a *garden*, Sand?
Sandy	Oh, très passé. The mind boggles.
Horne	What do you suggest?
Julian	Paving, that's the answer here – paving.
Horne	Crazy?
Sandy	Absolutely insane! Or you have your various types of stone.
Julian	Yes, you have your Florentine marble –
Sandy	Comes lovely in Florentine marble –
Julian	Or you have your ceramics.
Sandy	Oh, fabe ceramics – all hand done by a disciple of William Morris in Ladbroke Grove. Or, Jule, wait a minute, how do you see his patio?
Julian	Wait a minute, wait a minute, it's all happening in here. I've got it – terrazzo!
Sandy	Oh, fantabulosa! Yes – and then maybe I could do something wild with a couple of creepers up his trellis. Yes, yes! I'm beginning to see it now. Go on, Jule.
Julian	Er – let's see – what about something decadent? A sunken birdbath?
Horne	I'm afraid I don't know any sunken birds.
Sandy	Oh, bold! Yes, go on – it's beginning to sing to me now.

Julian	Don't rush me, don't rush me – it's beginning to come over me in waves. I see it as a miniature version of the piazza in Florence.
Sandy	Oh, it's a breakthrough! Mr Horne, he's broken through. No – no – wait a minute – no – it won't work –
Horne	Why?
Sandy	Well, you can't have a mock Tudor house with an Italianate piazza out the back.
Horne	Well, what do you suggest we do?
Sandy	Only one thing for it. The house'll have to come down!

BARRY TOOK and MARTY FELDMAN

CONSERVATORIES AND GREENHOUSES

I've never had a greenhouse. I find it quite embarrassing to admit this because I know that the really keen gardener spends a lot of time in the greenhouse potting, cutting and thinning the seedlings. I think because I came to gardening late I was frightened of the responsibility of a greenhouse. I remember the traumas of my childhood when someone let the heating go out or forgot to open the glass panes to let the air in. As I have become older I have tried to simplify life's problems so I doubt if I will get one now, but I admire well kept greenhouses, and their owners, tremendously.

A couple of hundred years ago a greenhouse was the name for what we should call a conservatory. I haven't got one of those either! But I think I could be persuaded . . . if Annie promises to shoulder the burden.

My greenhouse is never so pleasant as when we are just upon the point of being turned out of it. The gentleness of the autumnal suns, and the calmness of this latter season, make it a much more agreeable retreat than we ever find it in summer; when, the winds being generally brisk, we cannot cool it by admitting a sufficient quantity of air, without being at the same time incommoded by it. But now I sit with all the windows and door wide open, and am regaled with the scent of every flower in a garden as full of flowers as I have known how to make it. We keep no bees, but if I lived in a hive I should hardly hear more of their music. All the bees in the neighbourhood resort to a bed of mignonette, opposite to the window, and pay me for the honey they get out of it by a hum, which, though rather monotonous, is as agreeable to my ear as the whistling of my linnets. All the sounds that nature utters are delightful – at least in this country.

WILLIAM COOPER to REVEREND JOHN NEWTON
18 September 1784

48

My Dear William,
Our severest winter, commonly called the spring, is now over, and I
find myself seated in my favourite recess, the greenhouse. In such a
situation, so silent, so shady, where no human foot is heard, and
where only my myrtles presume to peep in at the window, you may
suppose I have no interruption to complain of, and that my thoughts
are perfectly at my command. But the beauties of the spot are
themselves an interruption; my attention is called upon by those
very myrtles, by a double row of grass pinks just beginning to
blossom, and by a bed of beans already in bloom; and you are to
consider it, if you please, as no small proof of my regard that though
you have so many powerful rivals, I disengage myself from them all,
and devote this hour entirely to you ...

Letters of William Cowper

Who loves a garden loves a greenhouse too.
Unconscious of a less propitious clime,
There blooms exotic beauty, warm and snug.

WILLIAM COWPER *The Task*
1785

A morning of brilliant light swiftly showed how great a disaster it was. The garden appeared to be full of dying swans: every tulip had its long curved neck on the ground. In the meadow beyond the garden a great line of Turkey oaks, of an age certainly not less than two hundred and fifty years, that only twenty four hours before had seemed to shimmer with gold-green light, were now blighted to a hideous tobacco brown. I lacked the courage to look out at the tender shoots of roses, clematis, wisteria and a dozen other things. Even the flowers of *Primula denticulata*, both purple and white, were struck too into the attitude of dying, weeping swans, an attitude from which, like the tulips, they did not recover until late afternoon. One felt that the full cup of spring had been savagely snatched from one's lips by a callously evil hand, all the labours of winter and autumn being suddenly in vain. Mournfully I remembered my thirtieth birthday, May 16, 1935, when a disaster of even greater magnitude struck with twenty degrees of frost, burning every leaf of every tree with a bleak, black pestilence from which there was really no recovery all that summer.

It is at times such as this that one rushes to the greenhouse, as into the warm arms of a nurse, for comfort.

H E Bates *A Love of Flowers*
1971

COOLING OFF IN THE ICE HOUSE

Sir,
There is an ice house cut into the rock at the back of Ruskin's old home, Brantwood. When I was a boy an old outdoor servant of Ruskin called Wilkinson, lived at the lodge there. He told me that when Ruskin became crotchety and disturbed towards the end of his life, Mrs Severn his cousin would have him wheeled in there to cool off. Yours faithfully . . .

MR GRAHAM BINNS to *The Times*
September 1980

Mr Binns made the point to me that most ice houses are built in a way that could not accommodate a wheelchair, unlike the one in Ruskin's garden which was cut into the rock. Lucky really as I imagine a lot of troublesome elderly relatives might have come in for the same sort of treatment.

COUNTRY HOUSES

It is a rare creature who hasn't occasionally longed, like Malvolio, for the grandeur of a stately home set in a perfect park. We shuffle around a beautiful National Trust house and saunter through the grounds. Afterwards, over cream tea in the stable block, we imagine what it would be like to be master of all we have just surveyed. I see myself easily as a solid country squire in Jane Austen's nice country house, or a suave man about town extolling the virtues of my country seat to the tantalizing Zuleika Dobson. I suspect the sense of power over a huge garden would go to my head, though I hope I would show a little more restraint than George Sitwell, whose manic approach to landscaping is described here by his son, Osbert.

MY FATHER'S GARDEN

If he could not write about gardens with success, at least he could make them in the world of actuality. He abolished small hills, created lakes, and particularly liked now to alter the levels at which full-grown trees were standing. Two old yew trees in front of the dining-room windows at Renishaw were regularly heightened and lowered; a process which I then believed could have been shown to chart, like a thermometer, the temperature of his mood, and to which he always referred as 'pulling and dragging'. ('That oak tree needs to be pulled and dragged!') From the wooden towers constructed for the purpose in the lake and on the hill he would measure and survey. His head throbbed with ideas, the majority of them never to be put into practice. Glass fountains, aqueducts in rubble, gigantic figures, cascades through the woods, stone boats and dragons in the water of lake and pool, blue-stencilled white cows 'to give distinction to the landscape', many of these schemes, alas, remained where they were born. But they were a fine exercise for him, and a diversion.

OSBERT SITWELL

PARADISE

It puzzles much the sages' brains,
    Where Eden stood of yore;
Some place it in Arabia's plains;
    Some say it is no more.

But Cobham can these tales confute,
    As all the curious know;
For he had prov'd beyond dispute,
    That Paradise is Stowe.

NATHANIEL COTTON

Delaford is a nice place, I can tell you; exactly what I call a nice old-fashioned place, full of comforts and conveniences; quite shut in with great garden walls that are covered with the best fruit-trees in the country; and such a mulberry tree on one corner! Lord! how Charlotte and I did stuff the only time we were there! Then there is a dovecote, some delightful stewponds, and a very pretty canal, and everything, in short, that one could wish for; and, moreover, it is close to the church, and only a quarter of a mile from the turnpike-road. So 'tis never dull; for if you only go and sit up in an old yew arbour behind the house, you may see all the carriages that pass along. Oh, 'tis a nice place! A butcher hard by in the village, and the parsonage house within a stone's throw.

JANE AUSTEN *Sense and Sensibility*

A COUNTRY SEAT

He drank his coffee at one draught, pushed back his chair, threw away the cigarette he had just lit. 'Listen!' he said.

Zuleika folded her hands on her lap.

'You do not love me. I accept as final your hint that you never will love me. I need not say — could not, indeed, ever say — how deeply, deeply you have pained me. As lover, I am rejected. But that rejection,' he continued, striking the table, 'is no stopper to my suit. It does but drive me to the use of arguments ... You, Miss Dobson, what are you? A conjurer, and a vagrant; without means, save such as you can earn by the sleight of your hand; without position; without a home; all unguarded but by your own self-respect. That you follow an honourable calling, I do not for one moment deny. I do, however, ask you to consider how great are its perils and hardships, its fatigues and inconveniences. From all these evils I offer you instant refuge. I offer you, Miss Dobson, a refuge more glorious and more augustly gilded than you, in your airiest flights of fancy, can ever have hoped for or imagined. I own about 340,000 acres. My town residence is in St James's Square. Tankerton, of which you may have seen photographs, is the chief of my country seats. It is a Tudor house, set on the ridge of a valley. The valley, its park, is halved by a stream so narrow that the deer leap across. The gardens are estraded upon the slope. Round the house runs a wide paven terrace. There are always two or three peacocks trailing their sheathed feathers along the balustrade, and stepping how stiffly! as though they had just been unharnessed from Juno's chariot. Two flights of shallow steps lead down to the flowers and fountains. Oh, the gardens are wonderful. There is a Jacobean garden of white roses. Between the ends of two pleached alleys, under a dome of branches, is a little lake, with a Triton of black marble, and with water-lilies. Hither and thither under the archipelago of water-lilies, dart gold-fish – tongues of flame in the dark water. There is also a long strait alley of clipped yew. It ends in an alcove for a pagoda of painted porcelain which the Prince Regent — peace be to his ashes! — presented to my great-grandfather. There are many twisting paths, and sudden aspects, and devious, fantastic arbours. Are you fond of horses? In my stables of pinewood and plated-silver seventy are installed. Not all of them together could vie in power with one of the meanest of my motor-cars.'

MAX BEERBOHM *Zuleika Dobson*

HYACINTH got up early — an operation attended with very little effort, as he had scarce closed his eyes all night. What he saw from his window made him dress as quickly as a young man might who desired more than ever that his appearance shouldn't give strange ideas about him: an old garden with parterres in curious figures and little intervals of lawn that seemed to our hero's cockney vision fantastically green. At one end of the garden was a parapet of mossy brick which looked down on the other side into a canal, a moat, a quaint old pond (he hardly knew what to call it) and from the same standpoint showed a considerable part of the main body of the house — Hyacinth's room belonging to a wing that commanded the extensive irregular back — which was richly grey wherever clear of the ivy and the other dense creepers, and everywhere infinitely a picture: with a high piled ancient russet roof broken by huge chimneys and queer peep-holes and all manner of odd gables and windows on different lines, with all manner of antique patches and protrusions and with a particularly fascinating architectural excrescence where a wonderful clock-face was lodged, a clock-face covered with gilding and blazonry but showing many traces of the years and the weather. He had never in his life been in the country — the real country, as he called it, the country which was not the mere ravelled fringe of London — and there entered through his open casement the breath of a world enchantingly new and after his recent feverish hours unspeakably refreshing; a sense of sweet sunny air and mingled odours, all strangely pure and agreeable, and of a musical silence that consisted for the greater part of the voices of many birds. There were tall quiet trees near by and afar off and everywhere; and the group of objects that greeted his eyes evidently formed only a corner of larger spaces and of a more complicated scene. There was a world to be revealed to him: it lay waiting with the dew on it under his windows, and he must go down and take of it such possession as he might.

He rambled an hour in breathless ecstasy, brushing the dew from the deep fern and bracken and the rich borders of the garden, tasting the fragrant air and stopping everywhere, in murmuring rapture, at the touch of some exquisite impression. His whole walk was peopled with recognitions; he had been dreaming all his life of just such a place and such objects, such a morning and such a chance. It was the last of April and everything was fresh and vivid; the great trees in the early air, were a blur of tender shoots. Round the admirable house he revolved repeatedly, catching every aspect and feeling every value, feasting on the whole expression. . . . There was something in the way the grey walls rose from the green lawn that brought tears to his eyes. . . .

HENRY JAMES *The Princess Casamassima*

CUCKOOS

For years there's been a running joke in *The Times* about hearing the first cuckoo in spring. I never quite knew why, although it is true that the mere word 'cuckoo' is rather ridiculous. Then I was idly dipping into a collection of letters to *The Times* dating back to the beginning of the century and Eureka! all was clear. I am full of admiration for the unimpeachable honesty of Mr Lydekker in putting the record straight. I feel you can almost see his stiff upper lip as he composes himself to reveal all.

ON HEARING THE FIRST CUCKOO

Sir,

While gardening this afternoon I heard a faint note which led me to say to my under-gardener, who was working with me. 'Was that the cuckoo?' Almost immediately afterwards we both heard the full double note of a cuckoo, repeated either two or three times – I am not quite sure which. The time was 3.40; and the bird, which was to the westward – that is to say, to windward – appeared to be about a quarter of a mile away. There is not the slightest doubt that the song was that of a cuckoo.

The late Professor Newton, in the fourth edition of Yarrell's 'British Birds' (Vol. II., p. 389, note), stated that although the arrival of the cuckoo has frequently been reported in March or even earlier, such records must be treated with suspicion, if not with incredulity. And Mr J E Harting ('Handbook of British Birds,' p. 112) goes even further than this, stating that there is no authentic record of the arrival of the cuckoo in this country earlier than April 6.

Sir,

    I regret to say that, in common with many other persons, I have been completely deceived in the matter of the supposed cuckoo of February 4. The note was uttered by a bricklayer's labourer at work on a house in the neighbourhood of the spot whence the note appeared to come. I have interviewed the man, who tells me that he is able to draw cuckoos from considerable distances by the exactness of his imitation of their notes, which he produces without the aid of any instrument.

MR R LYDEKKER to *The Times*
6 and 12 February 1913

I am rather taken with these two fetching little ditties – his and hers cuckoo songs.

CUCKOO

The cuckoo's a fine bird,
He sings as he flies;
He brings us good tidings,
And tells us no lies.

He sucks little birds' eggs,
To make his voice clear:
and when he sings 'Cuckoo!'
The summer is near.

ANON

THE CUCKOO

O the cuckoo she's a pretty bird,
   She singeth as she flies,
She bringeth good tidings,
   She telleth no lies.

She sucketh white flowers
   For to keep her voice clear,
And the more she singeth cuckoo
   The summer draweth near.

ANON

A GARDENER'S CURSE

Awake my Muse, bring bell and book
To curse the hand that cuttings took.
May every sort of garden pest
His little plot of ground infest
Who stole the plants from Inverewe,
From Falkland Palace, Crathes too.
Let caterpillars, capsid bugs,
Leaf-hoppers, thrips, all sorts of slugs,
Play havoc with his garden plot,
And a late frost destroy the lot.

LADY MACONOCHIE OF INVEREWE

DAFFODILS

When I started getting really interested in gardening I quickly discovered the wonderful and easily achievable effect of a mass of daffodils clustering around the base of a tree. Since then I have been a keen fan of these amenable plants, which give so much delight to the eye with so little effort on the gardener's part. I do not fuss too much about which type of daffodil I use, unless they are to be in a bed close to the house and adjacent to other plants. I simply make a note each spring of an area which seems rather forlorn and empty and in the autumn I make sure I plant a good number of cheap and cheerful daffodil bulbs. Every year, as they naturalize and spread and their visual impact increases, I find I love them more.

Having indulged myself with Keats's *To Autumn* earlier on I am resisting the temptation to include Wordsworth's poem on the subject of daffodils. Instead here is a shorter but equally beautiful poem by Herrick.

TO DAFFODILS

Fair Daffodils, we weep to see
You haste away so soon;
As yet the early-rising Sun
Has not attained his noon
Stay, stay
Until the hasting day
Has run
But to the even-song
And, having pray'd together, we
Will go with you along.

We have short time to stay, as you,
We have as short a Spring;
As quick a growth to meet decay
As you, or any thing.
We die,
As your hours do, and dry
Away
Like to the Summer's rain;
Or as the pearles of morning's dew
Ne'er to be found again.

ROBERT HERRICK

DAMSONS

A damson tree is a marvellous addition to any garden. It has the prettiest white blossom in the spring, it produces delicious fruit and it doesn't grow too large for the average back garden.

I have always been particularly fond of damsons. My mother used to make that wonderful thick jam called damson cheese. It's not just the taste but the brilliant rich colour which makes damsons so special. Just a few damsons mixed in with a more pedestrian apple purée really lifts the whole pie or pudding into another league.

Trust Mrs Beeton to 'know everything there is to be knowed' about damsons. Until I read what she had to say I had no idea that this little plum originally comes from Syria and is named after the city of Damascus. As well as her thoughts on the damson I have included her recipe for a damson tart. The delicious flavour of the damson may be unchanging but you certainly couldn't match the cost today. By my reckoning 10*d* is 4 pence!

DAMSONS

Whether for jam, jelly, pie, pudding, water, ice, wine, dried fruit or preserved, the damson, or *damascene* (for it was originally brought from Damascus, whence its name), is invaluable. It combines sugary and acid qualities in happy proportions, when full ripe. It is a fruit easily cultivated; and, if budded nine inches from the ground on vigorous stocks, it will grow several feet high in the first year, and make fine standards the year following. Amongst the list of the best sorts of baking plums, the damson stands first, not only on account of the abundance of its juice, but also on account of its soon softening. Because of the roughness of its flavour, it requires a large quantity of sugar.

DAMSON TART

INGREDIENTS. — 1½ pint of damsons, ¼ lb. of moist sugar, ½ lb. of short or puff crust.

Mode. — Put the damsons, with the sugar between them, into a deep pie-dish, in the midst of which, place a small cup or jar turned upside down; pile the fruit high in the middle, line the edges of the dish with short or puff crust, whichever may be preferred; put on the cover, ornament the edges, and bake from ½ to ¾ hour in a good oven. If puff-crust is used, about 10 minutes before the pie is done, take it out of the oven, brush it over with the white of an egg beaten to a froth with the blade of a knife; strew some sifted sugar over, and a few drops of water, and put the tart back to finish baking: with short crust, a little plain sifted sugar, sprinkled over, is all that will be required.

Time. – ½ to ¾ hour.
Average cost, 10*d*.
Sufficient for 5 or 6 persons.
Seasonable in September and October.

MRS BEETON
1861

DEADLY
NIGHTSHADE

Not all plants and flowers are cosy and benign. How well I remember as a child my parents warning me about the Cuckoo Pint with its poisonous berries, and about the sinister plant with the sinister name – Deadly Nightshade. I believe women used to use the juice of the berries because the poison enlarged their pupils so that their eyes looked particularly beautiful and that is how it got its latin name of *belladonna*, beautiful lady. This piece from *The Go-Between* really conjures up the shudder I used to feel when I came across one of the plants my parents had warned me against.

'Wednesday 11th of July. Saw the Deadly Nightshade — Atropa Belladonna.'

Marcus wasn't with me, I was alone, exploring some derelict outhouses which for me had obviously more attraction than the view of Brandham Hall from the S.W. In one, which was roofless as well as derelict, I suddenly came upon the plant. But it wasn't a plant, in my sense of the word, it was a shrub, almost a tree, and as tall as I was. It looked the picture of evil and also the picture of health, it was so glossy and strong and juicy-looking: I could almost see the sap rising to nourish it. It seemed to have found the place in all the world that suited it best.

I knew that every part of it was poisonous, I knew too that it was beautiful, for did not my mother's botany book say so? I stood on the threshold, not daring to go in, staring at the button-bright berries and the dull, purplish, hairy, bell-shaped flowers reaching out towards me. I felt that the plant could poison me, even if I didn't touch it, and that if I didn't eat it, it would eat me, it looked so hungry, in spite of all the nourishment it was getting.

As if I had been caught out looking at something I wasn't meant to see I tiptoed away, wondering whether Mrs Maudsley would think me interfering if I told her about it. But I didn't tell her. I couldn't bear to think of those lusty limbs withering on a rubbish-heap or crackling in a fire: all that beauty being destroyed. Besides I wanted to look at it again.

Atropa belladonna.

L P HARTLEY *The Go-Between*

DESIGNING A GARDEN

Designing a garden is an exciting task. Most people don't have the opportunity to start completely from scratch. Time, expense and good sense means that most of us accept and adapt the garden we inherit when we arrive at a house. All the same the ideas put forward by inspired garden designers are worth reading and incorporating into your own garden when you have the chance, even if it has to be on a much smaller scale.

We start with the first great gardening writer (in my humble opinion) Francis Bacon. His thoughts, particularly on making sure the garden is a thing of beauty all year round, are as fresh today as they were nearly four hundred years ago.

FIRST STEPS

The garden is best to be square; encompassed, on all the four sides, with a stately arched hedge. The arches to be upon pillars of carpenter's work, of some ten foot high and six foot broad; and the spaces between of the same dimension with the breadth of the arch. Over the arches let there be an entire hedge, of some four foot high, framed also upon carpenter's work; and upon the upper hedge, over every arch, a little turret, with a belly, enough to receive a cage of birds; and over every space between the arches some other little figure, with broad plates of round coloured glass, gilt, for the sun to play upon. But this hedge I intend to be raised upon a bank, not steep, but gently slope, of some six foot, set all with flowers. Also I understand that this square of the garden should not be the whole breadth of the ground, but to leave, on either side, ground enough for diversity of side alleys; unto which the two covert alleys of the green may deliver you. But there must be no alleys with hedges at either end of this great enclosure: not at the hither end, for letting your prospect upon this fair hedge from the green; nor at the further end, for letting your prospect from the hedge, through the arches, upon the heath.

Sir Francis Bacon *Of Gardens*
1625

THE ALL YEAR GARDEN

I do hold it in the Royal Ordering of Gardens, there ought to be Gardens for all the Months in the year, in which, severally, things of Beauty may be then in season.

For December and January, and the latter part of November, you must take such things as are green all Winter: Holly, Ivy, Bays, Juniper, Cypress-Trees, Yews, Pine-Apple Trees, Fir-Trees, Rosemary, Lavender, Periwincle, the White, the Purple, and the Blue, Germander, Flags, Orange-Trees, Limon-Trees, and Myrtles, if they be striped, and Sweet Marjoram warm set.

There followeth, for the latter part of January and February, the Mezerion Tree, which then blossoms, Crocus Vernus, both the Yellow and the Grey, Prim-Roses, Anemones, the Early Tulippa, Hiacynthus Orientalis, Chamarïris, Frettellaria.

For March, there come Violets, specially the Single Blue, which are the Earliest, the yellow Daffadil, the Daisy, the Almond-Tree in blossom, the Peach-Tree in blossom, the Cornelian-Tree in blossom, Sweet Briar.

In April follow the double White Violet, the Wall-Flower, the Stock-Gilly-Flower, the Cowslip, Flower-de-Lices, and Lilies of all natures. Rosemary-Flowers, the Tulippa, the Double Piony, the pale Daffadill, the French Honey-Suckle, the Cherry-Tree in blossom, the Dammasin and Plum-Trees in blossom, the White Thorn in leaf, the Lelack Tree.

In May and June, come Pinks of all Sorts, specially the Blush-Pink Roses of all kinds (except the Musk, which comes later), Honey-Suckles, Strawberries, Bugloss, Columbine, the French Marygold, Flos Africanus, Cherry-Tree in fruit, Ribes, Figs in fruit, Rasps, Vine-Flowers, Lavender in Flowers, the Sweet Satyrion with the White Flower, Herba Muscaria, Lillium Convallium, the Apple-Tree in blossom.

In July come Gilly-Flowers of all Varieties, Musk-Roses, and the Lime-Tree in blossom, Early Pears and Plumbs in Fruit, Ginnitings, Quodlings.

In August, come Plumbs of all sorts in Fruit, Pears, Apricocks, Barberries, Filberds, Musk-Melons, Monkshoods of all Colours.

In September come Grapes, Apples, Poppies of all Colours, Peaches, Melo-Cotones, Nectarines, Cornellians, Wardens, Quinces.

In October and the beginning of November come Servises, Medlars, Bullaces; Roses Cut or Removed to come late, Hollyoaks, and such like.

These particulars are for the climate of London: But my meaning is perceived, that you may have *Ver Perpetuum*, as the place affords.

SIR FRANCIS BACON *Of Gardens*
1625

Creating a garden is like making music: the least distraction is apt to destroy the melodic line.

BEVERLEY NICHOLS *The Unforgiving Minute*
1978

Gardening. . . . In this the artist who lays out the work and devises a garment for a piece of ground has the delight of seeing his work live and grow hour by hour; and, while it is growing, he is able to polish, to cut and carve, to fill up here and there, to hope, and to love.

PRINCE ALBERT, who played a large part in designing the gardens
at Balmoral and Osborne House

Gertrude Jekyll has achieved gardening immortality for her design ideas. She is most famous for her use of colour in the garden and for the way in which she pioneered the 'natural' garden after the Victorian enthusiasm for bedding out in straight rows and bright colours. Here she sums up her gardening philosophy.

'PAINTING' WITH FLOWERS

I am strongly of an opinion that the possession of a quantity of plants, however good the plants may be themselves and however ample their number, does not make a garden; it only makes a collection. Having got the plants the great thing is to use them with careful selection and definite intention. Merely having them, or having them planted unassorted in garden spaces, is only like having a box of paints from the best colourman, or, to go a step further, it is like having portions of these paints set out upon a palette. This does not constitute a picture; and it seems to me that the duty we owe to our gardens and to our own bettering in our gardens is to use the plants that they shall form beautiful pictures; and that, while delighting our eyes, they should be always training those eyes to a more exalted criticism; to a state of mind and artistic conscience that will not tolerate bad or careless combination or any sort of misuse of plants, but in which it becomes a point of honour to be always striving for the best.

GERTRUDE JEKYLL *Colour Schemes for the Flower Garden*
1908

All gardening is landscape painting.

ALEXANDER POPE

Cyril Fletcher is a great entertainer. I love the daftness of the Odd Odes he wrote and performed. He is also an inspired gardener and a first rate gardening writer. With his wife, Betty Astell, he has created several gardens over the years and recently, when he opened his garden to celebrate his eightieth birthday, he found two thousand people queuing at the gate to look around. In this extract from his autobiography he demonstrates the sensitivity and love of colour and light which make him such a marvellous gardener.

TRICKS OF THE LIGHT

The shapes of everything will matter: a low group of shrubs here, and there a coniferous exclamation mark. There will be formal hedges and flowering hedges and vast expanses of lawn and tiny enclosed gardens. Secret gardens, lakes, formal ponds — different levels. You will even, if you are a really artistic gardener, worry about and contrive tricks of sunlight — shafts of light coming through woods and avenues and hedges to enhance foliage of differing colours or jets of animated water. Here is the sort of subtlety I mean: on your west wall, or a west-facing slope or some westering portion of your garden you will have copper maples and russet-barked pines, and dark red roses, and pink camellias, and peonies and berberis and dusky dahlias to catch the red rays of the setting sun, which will give such a magic luminosity to those shades of red you will stay out in this enchanted place until the near-dark will send you inside, and on the way in, the tobacco plants and night-scented stocks will remind you that there is even an added dimension to your garden: that of the scented darkness.

CYRIL FLETCHER *Nice One Cyril*

SUN AND SHADOW

Another of my reasons for planning that my garden shall come to its zenith in late summer and autumn is because, in fact, the sun is then past its zenith. The angle of light gets lower every day. 'Never look at your garden at midday,' a painter once said to me and I have never forgotten his words. In straight, strong perpendicular light flowers rarely look their best. As the angle of light changes and lowers in August so shadows lengthen and all colour and contrast is lovelier: so that eventually, when the michaelmas daisies are in full glory, heavy with butterflies, there are effects as of light seen through lace, of shadow heightening light and light deepening shadow.

H E BATES *A Love of Flowers*
1971

Enid Bagnold's *The Chalk Garden* is the only play I know where the type of soil is included in the stage directions (or in the title for that matter), but novels frequently have references to gardening. If you stay alert while reading you can pick up some useful gardening tips along with your literature. In the extract from *Elizabeth and her German Garden* the garden design sounds positively mouth-watering.

NOVEL IDEAS

We have been very busy till now getting the permanent beds into order and planting the new tea-roses, and I am looking forward to next summer with more hope than ever in spite of my many failures. I wish the years would pass quickly that will bring my garden to perfection! The Persian Yellows have gone into their new quarters, and their place is occupied by the tea-rose Safrano; all the rose beds are carpeted with pansies sown in July and transplanted in October, each bed having a separate colour. The purple ones are the most charming and go well with every rose, but I have white ones with Laurette Messimy, and yellow ones with Safrano, and a new red sort in the big centre bed of red roses. Round the semicircle on the south side of the little privet hedge two rows of annual larkspurs in all their delicate shades have been sown, and just beyond the larkspurs, on the grass, is a semicircle of standard tea and pillar roses. In front of the house the long borders have been stocked with larkspurs, annual and perennial, columbines, giant poppies, pinks, Madonna lilies, wallflowers, hollyhocks, perennial phloxes, peonies, lavender, starworts, cornflowers, lychnis, chalcedonica, and bulbs packed in wherever bulbs could go. These are the borders that were so hardly used by the other gardener. Spring boxes for the veranda steps have been filled with pink and white and yellow tulips. I love tulips better than any other spring flower; they are the embodiment of alert cheerfulness and tidy grace, and next to a hyacinth look like a wholesome, freshly tubbed young girl beside a stout lady whose every movement weighs down the air with patchouli. Their faint, delicate scent is refinement itself; and is there anything in the world more charming than the sprightly way they hold up their little faces to the sun? I have heard them called bold and flaunting, but to me they seem modest grace itself, only always on the alert to enjoy life as much as they can and not afraid of looking the sun or anything else above them in the face. On the grass there are two beds of them carpeted with forget-me-nots; and in the grass, in scattered groups, daffodils and narcissus. Down the wilder shrubbery walks foxgloves and mulleins will (I hope) shine majestic; and one cool corner, backed by a group of firs, is graced by Madonna lilies, white foxgloves, and columbines. Oh, I could dance and sing for joy that the spring is here.

COUNTESS VON ARNIM *Elizabeth and Her German Garden*
1898

DRINKING IN THE GARDEN

Drinking in the garden is delightful of course. Avoid lunchtime sessions as these develop into all day and night sessions when friends refuse, or are unable, to move. Pimms is an excellent drink for the garden but dangerously deceptive and can lead to *Falling Down in the Garden*. Always take the precaution of staying on soft grass. Avoid *hard* surfaces, patios etc. and above all never stand too near water.

Annie has two wonderful recipes for summer drinks in the garden. One is alcoholic and one is not. Both are delicious so take your pick.

PEACH PUNCH

2 ripe peaches
2 bottles still Moselle, well chilled
1 bottle sparkling Moselle, well chilled
Castor sugar to taste
A good supply of ice cubes

Peel and stone the peaches carefully. Cut them into small pieces and place them in a large bowl. If you have a proper punch bowl so much the better. Rest the bowl in a second, larger bowl or dish which you have filled with ice cubes.

Pour one bottle of the still Moselle over the peaches, add two tablespoons of castor sugar and stir very gently.

Cover the bowl with a teatowel or cloth and leave for 20–30 minutes for the wine to absorb the flavour of the peaches.

Add the second bottle of still Moselle, which you have kept in the fridge during this time.

Just before serving add the bottle of sparkling wine to the punch. Taste, in case you wish to add a little more sugar.

Serve the liquid in chilled glasses, but leave the fruit in the bowl.

Do not add ice cubes to the punch itself or it will become diluted and lose its flavour.

GINGERED FRUIT PUNCH

2 pints of ginger ale
½ pint pineapple juice
1 pint fresh orange juice
Juice of three lemons

1 pint strong, hot China tea
Sugar to sweeten
Oranges, lemons, mint for garnish
Ice cubes

This may sound a strange combination but once it has been chilled the taste of the tea disappears into the fruit juice and ginger ale, yet the fact it is there gives the punch that little extra something.

Mix the fruit juices with the tea and ginger ale. Add sugar to taste. Cool then chill thoroughly.

Serve garnished with slices of orange and lemon and sprigs of mint. Add ice cubes if desired.

EARTHWORMS

These are jolly useful little chaps although they don't look particularly fetching. I was alarmed to hear that our good old British earthworm is under threat from a newcomer to the scene who doesn't work anything like as hard. Every child at school knows how vital earthworms are for keeping the soil healthy, so I hope we will all rally to their defence if this threat proves real and not just a figment of my fevered imagination.

THE EARTHWORM

Who really respects the earthworm,
the farmworker far under the grass in the soil.
He keeps the earth always changing.
He works entirely full of soil,
speechless with soil, and blind.

He is the underneath farmer, the underground one,
where the fields are getting on their harvest clothes.
Who really respects him,
this deep and calm earth-worker,
this deathless, gray, tiny farmer in the planet's soil.

HARRY EDMUND MARTINSON
(from the Swedish, translated Robert Bly)

FLOWERS

Day after day fresh flowers like stars arise,
And all the turf breaks into laughing eyes.

Hymns Ancient and Modern

Flowers are like human beings, they thrive on a little kindness. But treat them harshly and they'll soon start to wilt and fade.

FRED STREETER

I call a plant excellent when it has the following virtues: that of being able to stand on its own legs without stakes, of producing flowers of great beauty for weeks on end and of showing incontestable grace of form.

H E BATES

THE BREATH OF FLOWERS

And because the Breath of Flowers is far Sweeter in the Air (where it comes and goes, like the Warbling of Musick) than in the Hand, therefore nothing is more fit for that Delight, than to know what be the Flowers and Plants that do best perfume the Air. Roses, Damask and Red, are fast Flowers of their Smells, so that you may walk by a whole Row of them, and find nothing of their Sweetness; yea, though it be in a morning Dew. Bays likewise yield no Smell as they grow, Rosemary little, nore Sweet-Marjoram. That, which above all others, yields the sweetest Smell in the Air, is the Violet, specially the White double Violet, which comes twice a year, about the middle of April, and about Bartholomew-tide. Next to that is the Musk Rose, then the Strawberry Leaves dying with a most excellent Cordial Smell. Then the Flower of the Vines; it is a little Dust, like the Dust of a Bent, which grows upon the Cluster in the first coming forth. Then Sweet-Briar, then Wall-Flowers, which are very delightful to be set under a Parlour, or lower Chamber Window. Then Pinks, especially the Matted Pink, and Clove Gilly-Flower. Then the Flowers of the Lime-Tree. Then the Honey-Suckles, so they be somewhat afar off. Of Bean-Flowers I speak not, because they are Field-Flowers. But those which perfume the Air most delightfully, not passed by as the rest, but being Trodden upon and Crushed, are three: that is Burnet, Wild-Time, and Water-Mints. Therefore you are to set whole Alleys of them, to have the Pleasure when you walk or tread.

SIR FRANCIS BACON *Of Gardens*
1625

Flowers are delicate things and if you handle them delicately they'll behave themselves splendidly. Just like well trained children you know.

FRED STREETER

THE GARDEN AT APPLETON HOUSE

See how the flowers as at parade,
Under the colours stand displayed;
Each regiment in order grows,
That of the tulip, pink, and rose.
But when the vigilant patrol
Of stars walks round about the pole,
Their leaves that to the stalks are curled
Seem to their staves the ensigns furled.
Then in some flower's beloved hut,
Each bee, as sentinel, is shut,
And sleeps so too, but, if once stirred,
She runs you through, nor asks the word.
 O thou, that dear and happy isle,
The garden of the world erewhile,
Thou Paradise of the four seas,
Which Heaven planted us to please,
But, to exclude the world, did guard
With watery, if not flaming sword, –
What luckless apple did we taste
To make us mortal and thee waste?
Unhappy! shall we never more
That sweet militia restore,
When gardens only had their towers
And all the garrisons were flowers;
When roses only arms might bear,
And men did rosy garlands wear?

ANDREW MARVELL

Of all things made by man for his pleasure, a flower garden has the least business to be ugly, barren or stereotyped, because in it we may have the fairest of earth's children in a living, everchangeful state, and not, as in other arts, a mere representation of them.

WILLIAM ROBINSON *The English Flower Garden*

THE GARDEN OF LIVE FLOWERS

This time she came upon a large flower-bed, with a border of daisies, and a willow-tree growing in the middle.

'O Tiger-lily!' said Alice, addressing herself to one that was waving gracefully about in the wind, 'I *wish* you could talk!'

'We *can* talk', said the Tiger-lily, 'when there's anybody worth talking to.'

Alice was so astonished that she couldn't speak for a minute: it quite seemed to take her breath away. At length, as the Tiger-lily only went on waving about, she spoke again, in a timid voice — almost in a whisper. 'And can *all* the flowers talk?'

'As well as *you* can,' said the Tiger-lily. 'And a great deal louder.'

'It isn't manners for us to begin, you know,' said the Rose, 'and I really was wondering when you'd speak! Said I to myself, "Her face has got *some* sense in it, though it's not a clever one!" Still, you're the right colour, and that goes a long way.'

'I don't care about the colour,' the Tiger-lily remarked. 'If only her petals curled up a little more, she'd be all right.'

Alice didn't like being criticised, so she began asking questions. 'Aren't you sometimes frightened at being planted out here, with nobody to take care of you?'

'There's the tree in the middle,' said the Rose. 'What else is it good for?'

'But what could it do, if any danger came?' Alice asked.

'It could bark,' said the Rose.

'It says "Boughwough!"' cried a Daisy. 'That's why its branches are called boughs!'

'Didn't you know *that*?' cried another Daisy. And here they all began shouting together, till the air seemed quite full of little shrill voices. 'Silence, every one of you!' cried the Tiger-lily, waving itself passionately from side to side, and trembling with excitement. 'They know I ca'n't get at them!' it panted, bending its quivering head towards Alice, 'or they wouldn't dare to do it!'

'Never mind!' Alice said in a soothing tone, and, stooping down to the daisies, who were just beginning again, she whispered 'If you don't hold your tongues, I'll pick you!'

There was silence in a moment, and several of the pink daisies turned white.

'That's right!' said the Tiger-lily. 'The daisies are worst of all. When one speaks, they all begin together, and it's enough to make one wither to hear the way they go on!'

'How is it you can all talk so nicely?' Alice said, hoping to get it into a better temper by a compliment. 'I've been in many gardens before, but none of the flowers could talk.'

'Put your hand down, and feel the ground,' said the Tiger-lily. 'Then you'll know why.'

Alice did so. 'It's very hard,' she said; 'but I don't see what that has to do with it.'

'In most gardens', the Tiger-lily said, 'they make the beds too soft — so that the flowers are always asleep.'

This sounded a very good reason, and Alice was quite pleased to know it. 'I never thought of that before!' she said.

Lewis Carroll *Through the Looking-glass*
1871

Dark-leaved arbutus blooms with wax-pale bells
And their faint honey-smells,
The velvety syringa with smooth leaves,
Gloxinia with a green shade in the snow,
Jasmine and moon-clear orange-blossoms and green blooms
Of the wild strawberries from the shade of woods.

EDITH SITWELL *The Swans*

FLOWERS

Children – we're going to do our nice 'Moving to Music' this morning, so let's make a lovely fairy ring, shall we? And then we'll all be flowers growing in the grass.

Let's make a big circle – spread out – wider – wider – just finger-tips touching – that's it.

Sue, let go of Neville –

Because flowers don't hold hands, they just touch finger-tips.

SUE. Let go of Neville.

And Sue, we don't want GRUMBLERS in our fairy ring, do we? We only want *smilers*.

Yes David, you're a smiler – so is Lavinia – and Peggy and Geoffrey. Yes, you're *all* smilers.

QUIET, PLEASE.

Don't get so excited.

And Sue is going to be a smiler too, aren't you Sue? That's better.

George – don't do that . . .

Now then, let's all put on our Thinking Caps, shall we, and think what flower we are going to choose to be.

Lavinia? – What flower are you?

A bluebell. Good.

Peggy?

A red rose. That's nice.

Neville?

A *wild* rose. Well done, Neville!

Sidney? – Sidney, pay attention, dear, and don't pummel Rosemary – what flower are you going to choose to be?

A *horse* isn't a flower, Sidney.

No children, it isn't funny, it's very silly. If Sidney can't think of a better flower than that we'll have to go on to someone else until he can.

Now then Sue, what are you?

Another rose! Oh I *have* got a lovely bunch of roses, haven't I? Peggy is a *red* one and Neville is a *wild* one, so I expect you are a beautiful *white* one, aren't you?

Oh, you're another red one! I see . . .

Now then Sidney?

A carrot *isn't a flower*, Sidney. *Think* dear, and don't blow like that. How about a tulip?

A holly-leaf isn't a flower, Sidney. All right, you'd better be a holly-leaf.

Now, children, listen very carefully.

Elvis, stop bouncing, please.

No, bouncing isn't dancing, Elvis. Don't argue, dear – just stop bouncing. You watch the others – you'll see.

When Miss Boulting plays her music I want you all to get up on to your tipmost toes, light as feathers, and dance away all over the room where ever the music takes you. And remember: you are all lovely flowers in the grass.

Everybody ready?

Just a minute, Miss Boulting.

Sidney – come here, please.

What have you got in your mouth?

I can't hear a word you're saying, Sidney, so go out of the room and spit it out, whatever it is, and then come back and tell me what it was. And Sidney. Both feet. Don't hop.

Now then, children, we're not going to wait for a boy who puts things in his mouth like a baby – we're going to be lovely flowers growing in the grass, and the sun is shining down on us to make us grow tall and beautiful and – Geoffrey, stand up – flowers don't look backwards through their legs, do they?

What flower are you?

A fat daisy! Good.

Hazel, what do we do with our heads?

We hold them up.

I should think so.

Come in, Sidney!

COME IN. There's no need to knock the door down, is there?

Now what did you have in your mouth?

It can't have been nothing, Sidney, because I distinctly saw something.

Yes, I know it's nothing *now* but what was it *then*?

A big button! Well, I'm very glad you spat it out, aren't you?

You didn't? Do you feel all right, Sidney? Sure?

Well, get back into your place, then.

Incidentally, where did you get the button?

Off Rosemary's pink frock. I'm ashamed of you, Sidney, a big boy of four to go around eating buttons off little girls' frocks. What flower are you going to be? I've forgotten. You'd better be a hollyhock.

No, you can't be a *super-jet*, and if you are going to be a crosspatch you'd better go and sit down over there till you are a nice boy again. You can be thinking what flower you are going to be. Go along . . .

George – what did I say before? Well, don't . . .

Come along, children. Listen carefully to the music and then dance like a flower to it.

We're ready at last, Miss Boulting. I'm so sorry.

One – two – Off we go.

Dance, Neville, don't just stand there. Dance.

Head up, Hazel, and use your arms.

Peggy, dear – don't forget to breathe.

Rhythm, George. And cheer up – you're a *happy* flower, George. Yes, you are.

Because I say so.

Oh good, Sidney, I knew you'd think of something.

All right, you shall be a cauliflower – only be it *gently*.

JOYCE GRENFELL *George – Don't Do That*
1977

I have known many Persons of Fortune pretend much affection to Flowers, but very unwilling to part with anything to purchase them; yet if obtained by begging, or perhaps by stealing, contented to give them entertainment.

JOHN REA *Flora, Ceres and Pomona*
1665

THE NAMING OF FLOWERS

I always think what an enjoyable time the horticulturists must have naming new sorts of flowers, and how they must delight in compiling their catalogues. How fortunate, too, are all the people who are so lucky as to have flowers called after them – what could be more pleasing, for instance, than for Mrs Mark to go down to posterity remembered by a beautiful gladiolus, called after her, so charmingly, 'Mrs Mark's Memory'?

It is a curious thing that in catalogues the names of roses always fit the people after whom they have been named. There is Lady Sylvia, 'dainty and fragrant, pink blushing to apricot', just as she should be, whereas, on the other hand, Lady Forteviot is, as she *sounds* to be, 'robust, golden yellow deepening to rich apricot'. Lady Forteviot is a strong rose, a rose of character; it is not at all surprising to learn that she is 'mildew-resisting'. Emma Wright also is mildew-resisting. Emma has a homely practical name, and we understand how stalwartly she would resist attacks from mildew. We are not surprised, either, to find that Christopher Stone is 'Vigorous and upright in growth', but we are sad to see that George Dickson mildews badly, and that he is a vivid blackish crimson. On the other hand, the Rev F Page Roberts is, though sometimes shaded, very fragrant, and Mr W E Chaplin is 'of perfect shape'.

The ladies Poulsen are all bright scarlet; Karen, one learns, is not quite as tall as Kirsten and Else; as for Little Dorrit, she is scented and does not sport; she is evidently prim and proper. But who was the Village Maid, whose rose is pale with darker stripes, and who, too, were the Great and Small maidens who blushed? How suitable it is that Cardinal Richelieu should be deep purple crimson – and double! How right, too, that Josephine, Napoleon's empress, who had the most superb collection of roses in the world at Malmaison, is left to us now in 'Souvenir de Malmaison', a rose that has – 'clear flesh; large, is superb in a hot season, and very fragrant'.

JONQUIL ANTONY *Mrs Dale at Home*
1952

THE VILLAGE FLOWER SHOW

. . . Now better days are returning. Marquees have reappeared and the big nurserymen in the county are again willing to show their wares. The sumptuous effect of the Best Box of Vegetables again graces the trestle tables, and how magnificent they are in shape and colour, those mixed collections of red tomatoes, orange carrots, ivory parsnips, pale potatoes freshly washed in milk, jade-green lettuce, blood-red beetroot, emerald peas, with one pod split open, and marrows like stranded whales.

How fine indeed, in their assembly, are the fruits of the earth, simply, and by cottagers displayed. Great hairy gooseberries set out on kitchen plates; blackcurrants the size of marbles; raspberries like pink thimbles made for a giantess; and some soft peaches and brown figs from the greenhouse of an Amateur-with-help. How rural are the eggs, the bunches of herbs, the home-made cakes, the coloured jars of jam, the golden honey. How pretty the baskets of mixed flowers, and how touching the jam-pots of wild-flowers and grasses collected by the children . . .

VITA SACKVILLE-WEST

Gwendolen	(Looking round.) Quite a well-kept garden this is, Miss Cardew.
Cecily	So glad you like it, Miss Fairfax.
Gwendolen	I had no idea there were any flowers in the country.
Cecily	Oh, flowers are as common here, Miss Fairfax, as people are in London.

OSCAR WILDE *The Importance of Being Earnest*
1895

All the wars of the world, all the Caesars, have not the staying power of a lily in a cottage garden. . . . The immortality of marbles and of miseries is a vain, small thing compared to the immortality of a flower that blooms and is dead by dusk.

REVEREND R J FARRER

FURNITURE

The best sort of garden furniture is, of course, made of chunky, natural hardwood which weathers well and is supposed to last for ever. This has two disadvantages. It tends to demand a biggish cash outlay and it might come from some part of the world where trees are being destroyed faster than they are being replaced. I got bored with that white plastic furniture which seems to be everywhere nowadays. It seems more appropriate for a hotter climate than ours and on our rare brightly sunny days I find it gives off a rather uncomfortable glare. What's the answer? Well I recently discovered olive-green plastic furniture. It's practical and ecologically sound and it blends in better with the foliage than the white version. So that's a problem solved and I hope my furniture stands the test of time a bit better than the garden seat in Hardy's poem.

THE GARDEN SEAT

Its former green is blue and thin,
And its once firm legs sink in and in;
Soon it will break down unaware,
Soon it will break down unaware.

At night when reddest flowers are black
Those who once sat thereon come back;
Quite a row of them sitting there,
Quite a row of them sitting there.

With them the seat does not break down,
Nor winter freeze them, nor floods drown,
For they are as light as upper air,
They are as light as upper air!

THOMAS HARDY

C. W. SHEERES. sc.

GARDENS

My garden will never make me famous,
I'm a horticultural ignoramus.

OGDEN NASH

The story of mankind started in a garden and ended in revelations.

OSCAR WILDE

Before you put this book away,
Please promise me that you will never say:
'You should have seen my garden yesterday.'

REGINALD ARKELL *Green Fingers*
1934

The Garden that is finished is dead.

H E BATES

WHAT IS A GARDEN?

Let us, then, begin by defining what a garden is, and what it ought to be. It is a piece of ground fenced off from cattle, and appropriated to the use and pleasure of man: it is or ought to be, cultivated and enriched by art, with such products as are not natural to this country, and, consequently, it must be artificial in its treatment, and may, without impropriety, be so in its appearance; yet, there is so much of littleness in art, when compared with nature, that they cannot well be blended; it were, therefore, to be wished, that the exterior of a garden should be made to assimilate with park scenery, or the landscape of nature; the interior may then be laid out with all the variety, contrast, and even whim, that can produce pleasing objects to the eye.

HUMPHRY REPTON *Observations on the Theory and Practice of*
Landscape Gardening
1803

My garden sweet, enclosed with walls strong,
Embanked with benches to sit and take rest
The knotts so enknotted it cannot be exprest
With arbours and alyes so pleasant and dulce
The pestilent ayers with flavours to repulse.

GEORGE CAVENDISH
1500–61

A garden is a lovesome thing, God wot!
Rose plot,
Fringed pool,
Ferned grot –
The veriest school
Of peace; and yet the fool
Contends that God is not –
Not God! in gardens when the eve is cool?
Nay, but I have a sign;
'Tis very sure God walks in mine.

REVEREND T E BROWN *My Garden*
1875

I find the love of garden grows upon me as I grow older more and
more.

MARIA EDGEWORTH
1767–1849

MY GARDEN

The pride of my heart and the delight of my eyes is my garden. Our house, which is in dimensions very like a bird-cage, and might, with almost equal convenience, be laid on a shelf or hung up in a tree, would be utterly unbearable in wet weather were it not that we have a retreat out of doors, and a very pleasant retreat it is. To make my readers comprehend it I must describe our whole territories.

Fancy a small plot of ground with a pretty, low, irregular cottage at one end; a large granary, divided from the dwelling by a little court running along one side; and a long thatched shed, open towards the garden, and supported by wooden pillars, on the other. The bottom is bounded half by an old wall and half by an old paling, over which we see a pretty distance of woody hills. The house, granary, wall, and paling, are covered with vines, cherry-trees, roses, honeysuckles, and jessamines, with great clusters of tall hollyhocks running up between them; a large elder overhanging the little gate, and a magnificent bay-tree, such a tree as shall scarcely be matched in these parts, breaking with its beautiful conical form the horizontal lines of the buildings. This is my garden; and the long pillared shed, the sort of rustic arcade, which runs along one side, parted from the flower-beds by a row of geraniums, is our out-of-door drawing-room.

I know nothing so pleasant as to sit there on a summer afternoon, with the western sun flickering through the great elder-tree, and lighting up our gay parterres, where flowers and flowering shrubs are set as thick as grass in a field, a wilderness of blossom, interwoven, intertwined, wreathy, garlandy, profuse beyond all profusion, where we may guess that there is such a thing as mould, but never see it. I know nothing so pleasant as to sit in the shade of that dark bower, with the eye resting on that bright piece of colour, lighted so gloriously by the evening sun, now catching a glimpse of the little birds as they fly rapidly in and out of their nests – for there are always two or three birds'-nests in the thick tapestry of cherry-trees, honeysuckles, and china-roses, which cover our walls – now tracing the gay gambols of the common butterflies as they sport around the dahlias; now watching that rarer moth, which the country people, fertile in pretty names, call the beebird; that bird-like insect, which flutters in the hottest days over the sweetest flowers, inserting its long proboscis into the small tube of the jessamine, and hovering over the scarlet blossom of the geranium, whose bright colour seems reflected on its own feathery breast: that insect which seems so thoroughly a creature of the air, never at rest; always, even when feeding, self-poised and self-supported, and

whose wings, in their ceaseless motion, have a sound so deep, so
full, so lulling, so musical. Nothing so pleasant as to sit amid that
mixture of rich flowers and leaves, watching the bee-bird! Nothing
so pretty to look at as my garden!

Miss Mitford *Our Village*

AN IRREGULAR GARDEN

I am one, you must know, who is looked upon as a humorist in
gardening. I have several acres about my house, which I call my
garden, and which a skilful gardener would not know what to call.
It is a confusion of kitchen and parterre, orchard and flower-garden,

which lie so mixt and interwoven with one another, that if a foreigner, who had seen nothing of our country, should be conveyed into my garden at his first landing, he would look upon it as a natural wilderness, and one of the uncultivated parts of our country. My flowers grow up in several parts of the garden in the greatest luxuriancy and profusion. I am so far from being fond of any particular one, by reason of its rarity, that if I meet with any one in a field which pleases me, I give it a place in my garden. By this means, when a stranger walks with me, he is surprised to see large spots of ground covered with ten thousand different colours, and has often singled out flowers he might have met with under a common hedge, in a field, or in a meadow, as some of the greatest beauties of the place. The only method I observe in this particular, is to range in the same quarter the products of the same season, that they may make their appearance together, and compose a picture of the greatest variety. There is the same irregularity in my plantations, which run into as great a wilderness as their natures will permit. I take in none that do not naturally rejoice in the soil; and am pleased, when I am walking, in a labyrinth of my own raising, not to know whether the next tree I shall meet with is an apple or an oak; an elm or a pear tree.

JOSEPH ADDISON *The Spectator*

Fair houses are more frequent than fine gardens; the first effected by artificers, the latter requiring more skill in their owner.

JOHN REA *Flora, Ceres and Pomona*
1665

A garden is like those pernicious machineries which catch a man's coat-skirt or his hand, and draw in his arm, his leg, and his whole body to irresistible destruction.

RALPH WALDO EMERSON

A garden is a thing of beauty and a job for ever.

Take it from us, it is utterly forbidden to be half-hearted about Gardening. You have got to LOVE your garden, whether you like it or not.

W C SELLAR and R J YEATMAN *Garden Rubbish*
1936

THE GARDEN

What wond'rous life is this I lead!
  Ripe apples drop about my head;
  The luscious clusters of the vine
Upon my mouth do crush their wine;
  The nectarine, and curious peach,
Into my hands themselves do reach;
  Stumbling on melons, as I pass,
Insnar'd with flowers, I fall on grass.

ANDREW MARVELL

God Almighty first planted a Garden; and indeed it is the purest of humane pleasures.

Sir Francis Bacon

It is a blessed sort of work, and if Eve had had a spade in Paradise and known what to do with it, we should not have had all that sad business of the apple.

Countess von Arnim *Elizabeth and her German Garden*
1898

ENGLAND AS A GARDEN

(The Duke of York's garden. The Queen and Ladies hidden. Enter a gardener and two servants.)

GARDENER: Go, bind thou up yon dangling apricocks,
Which, like unruly children, make their sire
Stoop with oppression of their prodigal weight:
Give some supportance to the bending twigs.
Go thou, and like an executioner,
Cut off the heads of too fast growing sprays,

That look too lofty in our commonwealth:
All must be even employ'd I will go root away
The noisome weeds, that without profit suck
The soil's fertility from wholesome flowers.

FIRST SERVANT: Why should we in the compass of a pale
Keep law and form and due proportion,
Showing, as in a model, our firm estate,
When our sea-walled garden, the whole land,
Is full of weeds, her fairest flowers chok'd up,
Her fruit-trees all unprun'd, her hedges ruin'd,
Her knots disorder'd, and her wholesome herbs
Swarming with caterpillars?

GARDENER: Hold thy peace:
He that hath suffer'd this disorder'd spring
Hath now himself met with the fall of leaf;
The weeds that his broad-spreading leaves did shelter;
That seem'd in eating him to hold him up,
Are pluck'd up root and all by Bolingbroke.

WILLIAM SHAKESPEARE *Richard II*

THE GLORY OF THE GARDEN

Our England is a garden that is full of stately views,
Of borders, beds and shrubberies and lawns and avenues,
With statues on the terraces and peacocks strutting by;
But the Glory of the Garden lies in more than meets the eye.

For where the old thick laurels grow, along the thin red wall,
You find the tool- and potting-sheds which are the heart of all;
The cold-frames and the hot-houses, the dungpits and the tanks,
The rollers, carts and drain-pipes, with the barrows and the planks.

And there you'll see the gardeners, the men and 'prentice boys
Told off to do as they are bid and do it without noise:
For, except when seeds are planted and we shout to scare the birds,
The Glory of the Garden it abideth not in words.

And some can pot begonias and some can bud a rose,
And some are hardly fit to trust with anything that grows;
But they can roll and trim the lawns and sift the sand and loam,
For the Glory of the Garden occupieth all who come.

Our England is a garden, and such gardens are not made
By singing:- 'Oh, how beautiful!' and sitting in the shade,
While better men than we go out and start their working lives
At grubbing weeds from gravel-paths with broken dinner-knives.

There's not a pair of legs so thin, there's not a head so thick,
There's not a hand so weak and white, nor yet a heart so sick,
But it can find some needful job that's crying to be done,
For the Glory of the Garden glorifieth every one.

Then seek your job with thankfulness and work till further orders,
If it's only netting strawberries or killing slugs on borders;
And when your back stops aching and your hands begin to harden,
You will find yourself a partner in the Glory of the Garden.

Oh, Adam was a gardener, and God who made him sees
That half a proper gardener's work is done upon his knees,
So when your work is finished, you can wash your hands and pray
For the Glory of the Garden, that it may not pass away!
And the Glory of the Garden it shall never pass away!

RUDYARD KIPLING

'You haven't a garden!' she cried scornfully. 'Then why are you an Englishman?'

CECIL ROBERTS *Gone Rustic*
1934

GARDENERS

I suppose I tend to think of all gardeners as old, gnarled, wise men of few words who lock into the rhythm of the seasons and take a long term view of life. But I've noticed that the gardeners, like the policemen, are getting younger. In London, where I tend my modest plot, there is a whole new breed of young, polite gentlemen and lady gardeners who rocket around the streets in little vans bringing help and support to townees who are overwhelmed by their own backyards. I'm inclined to think this a very good thing. It would be terrible if gardening became associated only with old men and sturdy women of uncertain years. When you get to know any of this new breed of gardener it's very reassuring to find that they have the same ingrained love of plants as the more conventional looking model.

With a little help from family and friends, I generally look after my garden myself. The exercise is good for a man who likes his food and drink. At times I long to hand everything over to a rustic treasure with a complete set of instructions. John Evelyn's list of daily tasks, written three hundred years ago, would fit the bill perfectly.

Every Monday Morning, he must walk about the whole place to observe what needs doing, what is amisse, before he does any other work . . . Make regular checks on beehives, seed and root boxes; clean, sharpen and repair tools in wett weather and put away every night. Stir heaps of dung and mould; clip hedges, mow lawns, prune fruit and murral trees and vines when stated. Ask every night what rootes, salading, garnishing will be needed next day, and bring it to cook in the morning and informe her from time to time what garden provision and fruite is ripe and in season to be spent . . . Gather and bring in all fruit . . . He may not dispose of any fruit or sell any vegetables, flowers or plants without first asking leave of master or mistress. He must show broken and worn out tools to the master before buying new ones.

JOHN EVELYN *Directions to his gardener at Saye's Court*
1687

THE LAST GARDENER

Kept all his life
an eye for beauty: the flame
of a rose in the morning sun,
dragonflies . . . and girls, the marble-sweet limbs
of brief-skirted girls delighted him.

Hates he nourished
fierce and blind: nasturtiums;
women in trousers; posh-talking men;
the fashion for hormones,
– and he couldn't abide cats!

Last of his line he lived to see
the pride of his life's work
bull-dozed for bungalows,
yet never succumbed
to the rust of regret.

Lived like an outlaw,
rough and free, in Woodbine Cottage,
the wreck behind the Natal Clinic:
died quiet as an oak
from a surfeit of time.

Fought Fate, its winds and its weeds,
for eighty years
but finally got carried off
by that ancient enemy of his,
a late April frost.

He won't be missed;
the one true artist in a village
levelled out to bland estates
with flowering shrubs and cocktail talk
and classes in pottery.

Stubborn as bindweed, cunning as ivy,
he picked up some pints
playing rustic to fools
but where his craft was concerned
was not to be moved.

The journeyman of Nature
respected its rules, would ever scorn
the trickster's ways to quick effect,
the skill in his hands
being honest and proud.

R A REEVES

The fair-weather gardener, who will do nothing except when wind and weather and everything else are favourable, is never a master of his craft.

CANON ELLACOMBE *In a Gloucestershire Garden*
1895

Come my spade. There is no ancient gentlemen but gardeners, ditchers and grave-makers; they hold up Adam's profession.

WILLIAM SHAKESPEARE *Hamlet*

Honour the gardener! that patient man
Who from his schooldays follows up his calling,
Starting so modestly, a little boy
Red-nosed, red-fingered, doing what he's told,
Not knowing what he does or why he does it,
Having no concept of the larger plan,
But gradually, (if the love be there,
Irrational as any passion, strong,)
Enlarging vision slowly turns the key
And swings the door wide open on the long
Vistas of true significance.

VITA SACKVILLE-WEST *The Garden*
1946

To a gardener there is nothing more exasperating than a hose that just isn't long enough.

CECIL ROBERTS

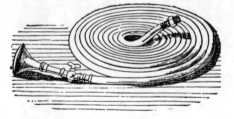

Garden Hose — Socks worn while you work in the garden.

Gardeners are good. Such vices as they have
Are like the warts and bosses in the wood
Of an old oak. They're patient, stubborn folk,
As needs must be whose busyness it is
To tutor wildness, making war on weeds.

GERALD BULLETT

WHY DOGS BITE GARDENERS

You mustn't think I'm not sorry for Lady Astor of Hever, because I am. It's no joke to break your foot and have to crawl about the estate, accompanied by three barking French whippets, until gardeners come to the rescue and wheel you to safety in a barrow. On the other hand, if you're a gardener loading a lady into a barrow, it's no joke to be bitten by three French whippets 'apparently thinking the gardeners were abducting their mistress'. Lord Astor, even, was moved to comment: 'It was hard luck to be bitten . . . but the men seemed to understand. We hadn't the heart to scold the dogs.'

My source of information is one of the more nobility-fancying

Press gossips, and as this particular piece carried news not only of the Astors but of the Queen, Prince Philip, Princess Birgitta of Sweden, Prince Johan of Hohenzollern, Sir Guy and Lady Shaw-Stewart, Sir Timothy Eden, Lord Downe, Lord Combermere and the Earl of Leicester, it was obviously impossible to introduce any sort of statement from mere gardeners. As Lord Astor said – avoiding any degrading suggestion of direct spokesmanship – they seemed to understand. The point I want to make is that the dogs didn't. They barked for help, and when help came they attacked it. It now gives me great pleasure to attack the dogs. The Astors may not have had the heart to scold them. I have.

These dogs, like all dogs, were fools. Admirers of the canine intelligence, so-called, tweedy folk of the 'he-understands-every-word-we-say' school, will be shocked to read this. And not before time. 'How lucky', they have been saying to each other, 'that the dogs were there to bark for help. And of *course* when those great rough gardener men came stamping round in their horrid gaiters they bit them. Why, poor little things, they must have been in an awful state.' I don't take this view. I take one or two others.

(a) The dogs weren't barking for help at all. They were just barking. This is the average dog's contribution to any already exasperating situation, and is one of many pointers to the essential dimness of the species. If the dog had any whit of the intelligence ascribed to him he would know that, for instance, any domestic crisis involving, say, dropped crockery or a bird catching fire on removal from the oven, would be a good time to get out of sight under the table and stay there. How many dogs have the intelligence to see this? Instead, they go into fits of yelping hysterics, showing the whites of their eyes and plunging into the storm-centre, where they trip people up and get their feet wedged in the vegetable-rack. Lady Astor's dogs were instinctively making a confounded nuisance of themselves. Either they resented her being on all fours, trying to get into their act, or they felt intuitively that she was in trouble, and that a concerted bout of shrill barking would stand a good chance of making things more difficult than they were already. Intelligence didn't come into it.

(b) Supposing, just for the sake of argument, that it did. Supposing they worked this thing out rationally.

1st FRENCH WHIPPET:	(*in French, but never mind*) Look chaps, Mistress has fallen down.
2nd FW:	How come? I wasn't watching.
3rd FW:	Tripped, I think. What's she saying?

1st FW:	Sounds like. 'oo, my foot.' She's starting to crawl. Ought we to get help?
2nd FW:	Pardon? Sorry, interesting smell here. Well, she won't get far at that rate. What about a good bark? Might fetch the gardeners.
3rd FW:	Not a bad idea. All set then?
All:	Row-row! Row-row-row! Row-row-row-row! Row-row-row (Etc).

How's that for a reconstruction, dog-lovers? Chime in with your theories all right, does it? Good. Then let's move forward in time about ten minutes. Dimly, above the canine SOS, feet are heard approaching through the undergrowth.

All FW's:	(*as before*) Row-row! Row-row-row-row! (Etc.)
1st FW:	Here come the gardeners, chaps.
2nd FW:	They've spotted her.
3rd FW:	They're lifting her up. Row-row-row!
1st FW:	Row-row!
2nd FW:	They've fetched a barrow. Row-row-row!
3rd FW:	Ready boys? They're putting her into it. Stand by to bite gardeners.
1st FW:	Bags I first. Grrr-rr-rr!
All:	Grrr!

They sink teeth into gardeners' calves, ankles, wrists, etc.
Of course, I realize I haven't a chance of swaying dog-lovers.

They'll soon find a way to explain and defend this sudden lapse from rational Good Samaritan into berserk fangster. One of the gardeners, no doubt, was wearing a jumble-sale hat, formerly the property of a Russian agent. Or the dogs had been following the Lady Chatterley case and feared the worst as soon as they saw a coarse hand laid on their stricken mistress.

Well, I'm sorry. I've nothing against dogs, any more than I've anything against the Astors. I just want to explode the intelligence myth, that's all. I've even got a dog of my own. His name's Spot, and you only have to mention a word that rhymes with it, such as clot or guillemot, and he's up from the hearthrug trying to get an imaginary biscuit out of the hand you're holding your glass in. Other indications of his having no sense whatsoever include seeing off the goldfish, thinking it's bedtime and cringing into his kennel in mid-afternoon when all you've suggested is a strategic walk around the garden, trying to go upstairs when two men are coming down with a wardrobe, jumping up for twenty minutes at a tennis-ball on a string plainly two feet out of range, not being able to find a bit of cheese-rind he's standing with his foot on, and barking his head off every night at six when I come home, still not knowing my footsteps from a Broadmoor fugitive's after seven years of hearing them every night at six.

Dogs are fools, but at least I know it. When mine finds me crawling home on all fours with a broken foot it won't surprise me at all if he sinks his teeth in the rescue party. The real surprise will be if he doesn't sink them in me.

BASIL BOOTHROYD

110

BE NICE TO YOUR GARDENER

I shall never forget a June evening when we went for a walk in the kitchen garden, which was immense and furnished with enough asparagus to feed battalions of orphans for months. Everything was immaculate; not a weed on the smooth surface of the cinder paths, not a trace of blight on the heavily laden broad beans. Suddenly Molly stopped in her tracks. There at her feet lay a small trowel which must have been left by one of the gardener's boys.

'Do you see,' said Molly in a strangled voice, 'what I see?'

I did indeed, and I bent down to pick it up.

'No!' she exclaimed. 'Do not touch it. Leave it alone!'

She might have been talking of a high explosive. But she was not looking at me, she was staring to the end of the path, down which Hawkins, the head gardener, was slowly approaching.

He came up to us and touched his cap.

'Good evening, Hawkins.'

'Good evening, m'lady.'

'This, Hawkins, is Mr Beverley Nichols.'

'Good evening, sir.'

'Mr Nichols is a very famous gardener.'

Hawkins made no comment on this assertion.

She pointed to the trowel. 'Is *this* the sort of thing we like Mr Nichols to see at Broadlands, Hawkins? Garden tools scattered all over the place?'

He bent down slowly and picked it up. When he straightened himself he was very red in the face. Again he touched his cap. 'Good evening, m'lady.'

Molly had given her little sting, and as with the bee, she had parted with something of herself in doing so. She was tired and dispirited when we walked back to the house, not with Hawkins but with herself. For she was, I repeat, a kindly woman at heart, and when she died she did something which must have made Hawkins forgive her for all her tiresomeness – she remembered him in her will.

Beverley Nichols *Garden Open Today*
1963

MAD GARDENER'S SONG

He thought he saw an Elephant,
  That practised on a fife:
He looked again, and found it was
  A letter from his wife.
'At length I realize,' he said,
  'The bitterness of Life!'

He thought he saw a Buffalo
  Upon the chimney-piece:
He looked again, and found it was
  His Sister's Husband's Niece.
'Unless you leave this house,' he said,
  'I'll send for the Police!'

He thought he saw a Rattlesnake
  That questioned him in Greek:
He looked again, and found it was
  The Middle of Next Week.
'The one thing I regret,' he said,
  'Is that it cannot speak!'

He thought he saw a Banker's Clerk
  Descending from the bus:
He looked again, and found it was
  A Hippopotamus:
'If this should stay to dine,' he said,
  'There won't be much for us!'

He thought he saw a Kangaroo
  That worked a coffee-mill:
He looked again, and found it was
  A Vegetable-Pill.
'Were I to swallow this,' he said,
  'I should be very ill!'

He thought he saw a Coach-and-Four
  That stood beside his bed:
He looked again, and found it was
  A Bear without a Head.
'Poor thing,' he said, 'poor silly thing!
  'It's waiting to be fed!'

He thought he saw an Albatross
    That fluttered round the lamp:
He looked again, and found it was
    A Penny-Postage-Stamp.
'You'd best be getting home,' he said:
    'The nights are very damp!'

He thought he saw a Garden-Door
    That opened with a key:
He looked again, and found it was
    A Double Rule of Three:
'And all its mystery,' he said,
    'Is clear as day to me!'

He thought he saw an Argument
    That proved he was the Pope:
He looked again, and found it was
    A Bar of Mottled Soap.
'A fact so dread,' he faintly said,
    'Extinguishes all hope!'

LEWIS CARROLL

A country parson without some knowledge of plants is surely as incomplete as a country parsonage without a garden.

CANON ELLACOMBE *In a Gloucestershire Garden*
1985

All gardeners know better than other gardeners.

Chinese proverb

The true gardener, like a true artist, is never satisfied.

H E BATES

HEAD GARDENER AT BUCKINGHAM PALACE

It is really wonderful what can be grown in a London garden. The lilies-of-the-valley are in profusion everywhere in the shrub borders, and the Queen Mother often asked for a bunch or two to be sent in to her boudoir, just as she did as a girl. Most of the flowers for house decoration, however, came in from Windsor every day; but it is the little homely touch of the lily-of-the-valley incident which shows how Her Majesty loves the simple flowers, and how she notices the humbler plants.

What a great shame it would be if our Royal Family did not have this quiet, unassuming, typically British garden to walk about in whenever they wished. One can indeed be very thankful for Buckingham Palace gardens.

One of the interesting things about being Head Gardener at Buckingham Palace is that you never know what is going to happen. For instance, a year or two back Mr Cole was called into the office of the Master of the Household to meet an American who had come over from the USA with three large rose bushes, of the variety Peace. He wished to present them to the King, and they were graciously received on His Majesty's behalf. The American friend was a member of the Rose Lovers' League, and was dressed in the uniform of that body. It was a special linen suit, light in colour, with a large embroidered badge on the left sleeve, and a straw hat with a special ribbon round.

This idea of members of horticultural societies having a special uniform, if it spread to England, might easily revolutionise the gardeners' meetings which take place all over the country. The Delphinium Society could choose light blue; the National Chrysanthemum Society a lovely bronze; the Succulent and Cacti Society, a dark green, without, I hope, the necessary thorns!

W E SHEWELL-COOPER *The Royal Gardeners*
1952

GARDEN PARTIES

Not parties in the garden but the real thing – the Buckingham Palace Garden Party. What an honour to be invited, just you and 8,000 of the Queen's closest friends. I doubt if I would be as tolerant as Her Majesty watching that number of people tramp across my lawn. Of course it's a real treat to see London's largest private garden with its *pièce de résistance* the deep herbaceous border where the formality is in such a contrast to the area which Prince Charles insists is kept wild and natural. The flamingos are great fun too. Although I didn't actually take tea with one of the royal family it was nice to have been asked and definitely something to recall in later years with the grandchildren. That's where a diary comes in so handy as others have found before me.

22 July 1945
At the Royal Garden Party Queen Mary was in a cloth-of-gold coat and looked magnificent, but ageing. A bit bowed, I thought, as she advanced slowly. Seeing me, she put out her hand but I could think of nothing to say – I am never particularly good at these impromptu meetings, and she smilingly passed on. Drino Carisbrooke who saw our meeting, whispered to me: 'My cousin May is rather over-dressed.' A curious way to describe Queen Mary.

HENRY 'CHIPS' CHANNON *Diaries*

GOOSEBERRIES

Extraordinary the British obsession with gooseberries. So many books have references to them and I even found a leading article in *The Times* on the subject. I wonder whether they haven't gone a little out of fashion recently. Too much hard work all that topping and tailing. I read somewhere that people aren't eating as many oranges because peeling them is such a nuisance so the sales people are desperately fighting back with ideas like ready-peeled, shrink-wrapped oranges for packed lunches. They really will breed bananas with zips at this rate.

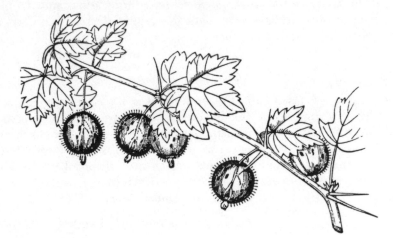

GOOSEBERRIES

AT this time of year a hundred years ago, or even fifty or less, a great many gardeners would be busy about their gooseberry bushes. A great many gardeners are still, of course, but those of the other days were altogether more anxiously employed. They would already, at an earlier season, have sternly thinned out the oncoming fruit, and under the swelling berries that remained they would now be regularly replenishing saucers of water, so placed to ensure that a moist atmosphere comforted the bush at all times. The enriched soil itself would be faithfully watered. And so in time some few enormous berries would be gathered in, for entry in the annual contest of one of those gooseberry clubs that flourished in the nineteenth century, especially in Lancashire, Yorkshire, and

Cheshire. The winning fruits were not, perhaps, of any remarkable flavour, but the members of the club got a deal of fun out of growing them and talking about them. 'It is to be regretted,' says the Royal Horticultural Society's *Dictionary of Gardening*, rather wistfully and not very hopefully, 'that such clubs have almost entirely died out, but perhaps in times of greater stability and greater leisure they may be revived and the benefits they confer upon a local community may be regained.' It would at least be better than growing bigger bombs.

The English language has been ungrateful towards the gooseberry. It deserves a better fate than that which has befallen 'sour grapes.' Everybody knows what 'playing gooseberry' is, and 'to play old gooseberry' — which is to play the deuce or generally make havoc — is not much better. The language does not faithfully reflect, as it should, the special place of the gooseberry in English horticulture — the way in which it flourishes in the land, the way in which it has been improved by cultivation here, the esteem in which it has long been held by all good British housewives. It has been left to a work compiled by M ANDRE SIMON to find words that do justice to the subject, that explain us to ourselves. 'The *Grande Cuisine* all but ignores gooseberries,' says the *Concise Encyclopaedia of Gastronomy*, 'but in England the selection, cultivation, and cooking of gooseberries have received a great measure of intelligent attention, and a boiled gooseberry pudding, made from young fruit no bigger than green peas, is one of the glories of English home cookery and an exquisite dish for all gourmets.'

It will soon be too late for gooseberry pudding, if the fruit is to be young enough for a gourmet, but there is time enough for other delights, and the beginning of June is a most suitable season for making gooseberry wine. This present generation, knowing very little about the subject, is apt to be loftily superior about gooseberry wine, but there are still connoisseurs about who praise it highly. The trouble is, they affirm, that beginners will not trouble to nurse it properly. The experts are not unanimous on this point, but some of them maintain that it should be left undisturbed for at least six months, and bottled only on a clear day, and then left undisturbed for many months more. Do the thing properly, they maintain, and your product may rival MRS PRIMROSE'S. DR PRIMROSE and his good wife, it may be recalled, had 'great reputation' for their gooseberry wine, and no passing traveller, refreshed by it, was ever known to find fault with it.

Fourth Leaders From The Times
1956–59

The Queen Mother has always been very fond of large, well coloured gooseberries for dessert.

W E SHEWELL-COOPER *The Royal Gardeners*
1952

A PERFECT PICNIC

Luncheon passed in almost unbroken silence. Both Zuleika and the Duke were ravenously hungry, as people always are after the stress of any great emotional crisis. Between them, they made very short work of a cold chicken, a salad, a gooseberry-tart and a Camembert. The Duke filled his glass again and again. The cold classicism of his face had been routed by the new romantic movement which had swept over his soul. He looked two or three months older than when first I showed him to my reader.

MAX BEERBOHM *Zuleika Dobson*

DOG BITES GOOSEBERRY!

And the raspberries and gooseberries! My Great-aunt had a favourite Aberdeen terrier, who, incredible though it may seem, loved ripe gooseberries. He used to sit up, as though he were begging, and eat them off the bush and wail aloud every few minutes whenever his nose was pricked.

ELEANOUR ROHDE *Herbs and Herb Gardening*
1936

GROTTOES – A COMMONSENSE VIEW

The Lincolnshire lady who showed him a grotto she had been making, came off no better, as I remember: 'Would it not be a pretty, cool habitation in the summer, Mr Johnson?' she said. 'I think it would, Madam,' replied he, '– for a toad.'

DR JOHNSON quoted by JAMES BOSWELL *Life of Johnson*
1781

HAPPINESS AND GARDEN HATERS

Being of the school of thought that believes happiness is a well-tended garden it came as a shock to come across the garden haters. My first experience of these characters was during a nostalgic journey back to my grandfather's suburban garden many years after his death. He had spent most of his long retirement in the garden, which was always immaculate. Its centrepiece was a lovely apple tree with mistletoe grafted on to it. There was a profusion of standard rose trees and a beautifully planted rockery surrounded by sweet smelling geraniums. I intended to photograph it in the colour it merited as I only had a few old black and white snaps to remind me of the happy times I had spent there.

I walked up and peered over the fence, my mind full of childhood memories. The first glimpse caused me to do one of my better double-takes and to check I had the right address. Yes, it *was* the right address, but where was the garden? There was no garden – just a scrubby patch of grass and a garage. Everything had gone – even the rocks from the rockery. A clear case of the dreaded garden haters.

I had a more recent sighting of one of these types who had cut down a fine tree in the spring and paved the area over because, as he informed me, 'It made such an awful mess in the autumn'! I firmly believe that those of the garden-hating tendency should be confined to flat dwelling.

What a relief to get back to people who take pleasure in their gardens.

To dig one's own spade into one's own earth! Has life anything better to offer than this?

BEVERLEY NICHOLS

Ah, yet, ere I descend to the grave,
May I a small house and large garden have;
And a few friends, and many books, both true,
Both wise, and both delightful too!
   And since love ne'er will from me flee,
A Mistress moderately fair,
And good as guardian angels are,
   Only beloved and loving me.

ABRAHAM COWLEY The Wish

If you would be happy for a week, take a wife. If you would be happy for a month, kill a pig. If you would be happy all your life, plant a garden.

Chinese proverb

The love of gardening is a seed that once sown never dies, but always grows and grows to an enduring and ever-increasing source of happiness.

GERTRUDE JEKYLL

There are people who go look at gardens and fountains while empires are being overthrown.

CHATEAUBRIAND

There are few greater pleasures in life than giving pleasure with a plant; or getting pleasure again with a plant. And certainly there is none more bland and blameless.

REVEREND R J FARRER *In a Yorkshire Garden*
1909

Vita to Harold   Sissinghurst

9 November 1948

Darling, it was such a lovely rich sunset this evening — the woods looked like tapestry, all brown and green, and the poplars on the way to the lake were bright gold. Then there was an extra bit of enchantment, because all the younger Jacob's sheep were playing a game round the big oak. They scampered round and round after each other, and sometimes they tried to run up the trunk of the oak, and then fell off again, and ran round again, and butted each other when they caught each other headlong. They played the game not knowing that I was watching them, all unselfconscious they were — it was like a Greek thing, an idyll, or like a frieze — it reminded me of Keats and the Grecian urn, only there was no urn, just our Sissinghurst field and the woods beyond.

Oh how happy I was — oh how happy — for that brief suspended moment. I felt so wildly happy that I had to tell you about it — like a sort of sharing.

Your Mar

Vita and Harold: The Letters of Harold Nicolson and
Vita Sackville-West
1910–62

THE GARDENER'S PRAYER

O Lord, grant that in some way it may rain every day, say from about midnight until three o-clock in the morning, but, you see, it must be gentle and warm so that it can soak in; grant that at the same time it would not rain on campion, alyssum, helianthemum, lavender, and the others which you in your infinite wisdom know are drought-loving plants – I will write their names on a bit of paper if you like – and grant that the sun may shine the whole day long, but not everywhere (not, for instance, on spiraea, or on gentian, plantain lily, and rhododendron), and not too much; that there may be plenty of dew and little wind, enough worms, no plant-lice and snails, no mildew, and that once a week thin liquid manure and guano may fall from heaven. Amen.

KAREL ČAPEK *The Gardener's Year*
1929

HARVEST

The idealized view and the modern reality!

... I thought myself very fortunate, one day last August, in being so near a five-barred gate, as to be enabled to escape from a cortege of labourers and harvest-waggons, sufficiently bulky and noisy to convoy half the wheat of the parish. On they went, men, women, and children, shouting, singing, and laughing, in joyous expectation of the coming Harvest Home, — the very waggons nodding from side to side, as if tipsy, and threatening, every moment, to break down bank, and tree, and hedge, and crush every obstacle that opposed them. It would have been as safe to encounter the Car of Juggernaut: I blest my stars for my escape, and after leaning on the friendly gate, until the last gleaner had passed, — a tattered rogue of seven years old, who, with hair as white as flax, a skin as brown as a berry, and features as grotesque as an Indian idol, was brandishing his tuft of wheat-ears, and shrieking forth, in a shrill childish voice, and with a most ludicrous gravity, the popular song of 'Buy a Broom.' ...

MISS MITFORD *The Rustic Wreath*

HARVEST HYMN

We spray the fields and scatter
  The poison on the ground
So that no wicked wild flowers
  Upon our farm be found.
We like whatever helps us
  To line our purse with pence;
The twenty-four-hour broiler-house
  And neat electric fence.

All concrete sheds around us
  And Jaguars in the yard,
The telly lounge and deep-freeze
  Are ours from working hard.

We fire the fields for harvest,
  The hedges swell the flame,
The oak trees and the cottages
  From which our fathers came.
We give no compensation,
  The earth is ours today,
And if we lose on arable,
  Then bungalows will pay.

All concrete sheds . . . etc.

JOHN BETJEMAN

HERBS

Herbs are wonderful for a gardener's ego. You can grow something really useful and delicious even if you have only a kitchen window sill. A large terracotta pot by the kitchen door filled with a variety of sweet smelling herbs and you are positively contributing to the happiness of nations. I began with a few everyday herbs but I've expanded my horizons considerably, especially as my wife likes to use a lot of herbs in her cooking. I recently tried to grow coriander and was rather cross when a kind friend pulled the little shoots out of the ground thinking they were an exotic weed. It doesn't do to be too insular when it comes to herbs, but I expect like most English actors he was influenced by Shakespeare's wonderful lines spoken by poor, mad Ophelia:

> There's rosemary, that's for remembrance. Pray you, love, remember. And there is pansies, that's for thoughts . . . There's fennel for you, and columbines. There's rue for you, and here's some for me. We may call it herb of grace o'Sundays. O, you must wear your rue with a difference. There's a daisy. I would give you some violets, but they withered all when my father died . . .

Such a beautiful speech, and not one word about coriander!

Mint has a wonderful taste and brightens up most things to which it is added. It is so easy to grow and of course it is delicious with new potatoes. These days it seems to crop up a lot as a garnish on puddings in fancy restaurants. Annie and I first came across mint used in salad at a summer party given by Leon Goossens, the famous oboist, and his wife Lesley.

MINTED SALAD

Take a handful of fresh mint leaves, washed and shaken dry.
Separate the leaves, use them whole if they are small, or tear them into small pieces. Mix well with whatever green salad leaves you are using and toss in a vinaigrette dressing just before serving.

Each generation believes it is the one which 'discovers' *everything*, from sex to the fact that things were much better in the good old days. Cooking is one of the skills which periodically gets 'discovered'. I have always enjoyed reading old books, particularly books about nature studies, which I collect. Annie has introduced me to the pleasures of dipping into old cookery books as well. It seems that healthy eating and adventurous ingredients have been around for centuries. Our medieval ancestors were awash with pasta and spices. The Victorians made a mean curry and John Evelyn in the seventeenth century knew a thing or two about putting together a salad. I was delighted when I found this recipe by a chef who worked for Charles II. I like to think that that excellent actress Nell Gwynn, Charles II's mistress, shared a plate of it with him. It certainly sounds colourful enough, being composed of fruit, flowers, salad leaves and, of course, that special ingredient that I thought I'd discovered for myself – mint.

ROBERT MAY'S SALAD

Take all manner of knots of buds of sallet herbs, buds of pot-herbs, or any green herbs, as sage, mint, balm, burnet, violet-leaves, red coleworts streaked of divers fine colours, lettice, any flowers, blanched almonds, blue figs, raisins of the sun, currans, capers, olives; then dish the sallet in a heap or pile, being mixed with some of the fruits, and all finely washed and swung in a napkin, then about the centre lay first sliced figs, next capers, and currans then almonds and raisins, next olives, and lastly either jagged beats, jagged lemons, jagged cucumbers, or cabbidge lettice in quarters, good oyl and wine vinegar, sugar or none.

ROBERT MAY *The Accomplisht Cook*
1660

I could not resist this extract from one of Ellis Peters's Brother Cadfael mysteries. They are set in the twelfth century, which I suppose really could claim with some truth to be the good old days. The monk's herb garden is an oasis of reassuring calm and his crusade against crime during the era of the Crusades makes wonderful reading for those well-earned moments in the garden deckchair.

BROTHER CADFAEL'S HERB GARDEN

Five minutes more, and he must go and wash his hands and repair to the church for Mass. He used the respite to walk the length of his pale-flowered, fragrant inner kingdom, where Brother John and Brother Columbanus, two youngsters barely a year tonsured, were busy weeding and edge-trimming. Glossy and dim, oiled and furry, the leaves tendered every possible variation on green. The flowers were mostly shy, small, almost furtive, in soft, sidelong colours, lilacs and shadowy blues and diminutive yellows, for they were the unimportant and unwanted part, but for ensuring seed to follow. Rue, sage, rosemary, gilvers, gromwell, ginger, mint, thyme, columbine, herb of grace, savoury, mustard, every manner of herb grew here, fennel, tansy, basil and dill, parsley, chervil and marjoram. He had taught the uses even of the unfamiliar to all his assistants, and made plain their dangers, too, for the benefit of herbs is in their right proportion, and over-dosage can be worse than the disease. Small of habit, modest of tint, close-growing and shy, his herbs called attention to themselves only by their disseminated sweetness as the sun rose on them. But behind their shrinking ranks rose others taller and more clamorous, banks of peonies grown for their spiced seeds, and lofty, pale-leaved, budding poppies, as yet barely showing the white or purple-black petals through their close armour. They stood as tall as a short man, and their home was the eastern part of the middle sea, and from that far place Cadfael had brought their ancestors in the seed long ago, and raised and cross-bred them in his own garden, before ever he brought the perfected progeny here with him to make medicines against pain, the chief enemy of man. Pain, and the absence of sleep, which is the most beneficent remedy for pain.

ELLIS PETERS *A Morbid Taste for Bones*
1977

Herbs are used for two purposes: a. to add a flavour that isn't there but should have been; and b. to take away a flavour that is there that shouldn't be.

WILLIAM RUSHTON *The Alternative Gardener*

In fennel-seed, this vertue you shall find
Foorth of your lower parts to drive the winde.

SIR JOHN HARINGTON *the Englishman's Doctor*
1608

HOSTAS

I find hostas a useful, workmanlike plants, ideal for my garden in what estate agents might call one of London's leafier suburbs. They are good plants if you suffer from allergies like hay fever, which make some of the more pollen rich flowers unsuitable for keen gardeners. This article from *Hortus* appeals particularly to my sense of humour, it's so unlikely it *must* be true.

TAKE ME TO YOUR HOSTAS

One Sunday, in the days of my youth, I was 'volunteered' with my younger brother to superintend the family garden which was opening up for a Red Cross Sunday. We had been weeding all morning, and at lunch time handed over to the various dignitaries who set up card tables, arrows to the lavatory, the tea tent and so on. Meanwhile, my brother and I lurked in the rhododendrons, ready to tackle cuttings pinchers, retrieve lost children, banish unwelcome dogs and generally see to the needs of the public. One of the first to arrive was a famous local Brigadier (retd.) who had a short fuse and tended to speak in telegrams. He obviously disliked teenagers intensely, for he glared at my brother and shouted 'Hostas!'

'Sorry?' queried my brother, who didn't know a dahlia from a damson.

'Where are your hostas?' The Brigadier's face was turning crimson. Clearly, with words at a premium he disliked having to repeat himself.

'They're not here, sir,' said my brother.

'Can see that! That's why I'm asking.'

'They've gone to India. They'll be back next week.'

'Good God!' said the Brigadier and strode off looking perplexed. I looked at my brother.

'What on earth did you say that for?' I asked.

'I thought "hosta" must be a military word for "parent".' He shuffled more deeply into the rhododendrons to hide his embarrassment. Inevitably, the military gent found the hostas and strode back to berate us.

'India be dammed!' he roared. 'Down by pond! Hostas! Dozens! Pretty sight. Love kalmias too! Very pretty. That boy your gardener? Useless! No clue!'

NIGEL COLBORN *Hortus*
1989

INSECTS
AND OTHER
CREEPY CRAWLY
CREATURES

I've already mentioned that I am a keen collector of old books on what used to be known as nature study. A particular favourite is *The Insect Legion* by Malcolm Burr for whom entomology (the study of insects) was, in his own words, 'the playmate of my boyhood and the mistress of my manhood'. His book is a positive mine of fascinating facts about insects.

He tells us of a species of beetle which has been found living quite comfortably thank you in the corks of the cyanide bottles which entomologists use for killing their specimens. There is a type of small black fly which is so chemically resistant it can live happily in crude petroleum.

Basically Dr Burr's frightening and well reasoned thesis was that man is only fooling himself when he thinks he rules the earth. 'Man's driving force is his Intellect. The driving force of the insect is *Life*.' Butterflies may be beautiful, bees may fertilize the plants and trees but insects also do terrible things; they eat our food, they spread disease, there are over 600,000 kinds of them and they are out to get us.

Well, it's a frightening prospect and the best I can do is endorse the words of Bill Vaughan, 'When the insects take over the world, we hope they will remember with gratitude how we took them along on all our picnics.'

'What sort of insects do you rejoice in, where *you* come from?' the gnat inquired.

'I don't *rejoice* in insects at all,' Alice explained.

LEWIS CARROLL *Through the Looking-glass*

The grasshopper, gnat and fly,
Serve for our minstrelsy;
Grace said, we dance a while,
And so the time beguile:
And if the moon doth hide her head
The glow-worm lights us home to bed.

ANON

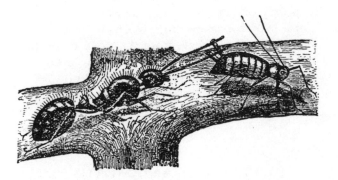

THE ANT

It appears from thence, that an Ant works as hard as a Man, who should carry a very heavy Load on his Shoulders almost every Day for the Space of four Leagues. 'Tis true, those Insects don't take so much pains upon a flat Ground; but then how great is the Hardship of a poor Ant, when she carries a Grain of Corn to the second Story, climbing up a Wall with her Head downwards, and her Backside upwards. None can have a true Notion of it, unless they see those little Animals at work in such a Situation.

JOSEPH ADDISON

ON THE GRASSHOPPER AND CRICKET

The poetry of earth is never dead:
  When all the birds are faint with the hot sun,
  And hide in cooling trees, a voice will run
From hedge to hedge about the new-mown mead;
That is the Grasshopper's — he takes the lead
  In summer luxury — he has never done
  With his delights; for when tired out of fun
He rests at ease beneath some pleasant weed.
The poetry of earth is ceasing never:
  On a lone winter evening, when the frost
  Has wrought a silence, from the stove there shrills
The Cricket's song, in warmth increasing ever,
  And seems in one to drowsiness half lost,
  The Grasshopper's among some grassy hills.

JOHN KEATS

BUTTERFLIES AND MOTHS

In this little book I want to tell you something about the common butterflies and moths which you may find in almost all parts of the country. But, first of all, I think that perhaps I had better say something about what we generally call their 'life-history.'

Of course you know that butterflies and moths are not butterflies and moths to begin with. They enter the world in the form of eggs, just as birds and fishes do. These eggs are often very beautiful indeed. You may find them on the leaves of different plants, sometimes on the upper side and sometimes on the lower side. And if you look at them through a good strong magnifying-glass — or, better still, through a microscope — you will find that some are shaped like little sugar-loaves, and some like acorns, and some like tiny melons, while they are nearly always covered with raised patterns which one might almost think must have been cut by fairy chisels.

In course of time these eggs hatch, and out come a number of little caterpillars, which at once begin to eat the leaves of the plant on which the eggs were laid. They have most wonderful appetites, and hardly ever stop feeding all day long. The consequence is, of course, that they grow very quickly; and in a few days' time they find that their jackets are much too tight for them. Then a most curious thing happens. Their skins split right down the back, and they wriggle and twist about, and rub themselves against the surrounding objects, till at last they manage to creep out of them altogether and appear in new ones, which had been gradually forming underneath the old!

Wouldn't it be nice if we could get new suits of clothes, or new frocks, as easily as this?

THEODORE WOOD *Butterflies and Moths Shown to the Children*

THE CENTIPEDE

There was a bee weighing down a blossom of thyme close by, and underneath the stalk a very ugly little centipede. The wild bee, with his little dark body and his busy bear's legs, was lovely to me, and the creepy centipede gave me shudderings; but it was a pleasant thing to feel so sure that he, no less than the bee, was a little mood expressing himself out in harmony with Design — a tiny thread on the miraculous quilt. And I looked at him with a sudden zest and curiosity; it seemed to me that in the mystery of his queer little creepings I was enjoying the Supreme Mystery; and I thought: 'If I knew all about that wriggling beast, then, indeed, I might despise him; but truly, *if* I knew all about him I should know all about everything — Mystery would be gone, and I could not bear to live!'

So I stirred him with my finger and he went away.

JOHN GALSWORTHY Inn of Tranquillity

THE SPIDER

On the wall appeared a spider, himself dark and defined, his shadow no less dark and scarcely if at all less defined.

They jerked, zigzagged, advanced, retreated, he and his shadow posturing in ungainly indissoluble harmony. He seemed exasperated, fascinated, desperately endeavouring and utterly helpless.

What could it all mean. One meaning and one only suggested itself. That spider saw without recognising his black double, and was mad to disengage himself from the horrible pursuing inalienable presence. . . .

CHRISTINA ROSSETTI Time Flies

A REMEDY AGAINST FLEAS

White wormwood hath seed, get a handful or twain
To save against March to make flea to refrain.
Where chamber is swept, and wormwood is strowne
No flea for his life dare abide to be known.

GEOFFREY GRIGSON An Englishman's Flora

KINGFISHERS

I've never seen one of these magical little birds in its natural habitat. Now that the salmon are returning to the Thames maybe it won't be too long before kingfishers become part of the London scene. Imagine tourists sending home postcards with pictures of kingfishers instead of red doubledecker buses. You never know.

February 1974   Reddish

The water-garden has become one of the most magical places in the garden. To visit this place of babbling water, and birds, is like being in a different country. To think that all these years I was hardly conscious that a river did go past my property! Every sort of bird seems to congregate here, quite different from those that come to the terrace. We are surprised often to see a heron or two on the lookout for fish. But the greatest excitement is a kingfisher – a rare enough streak of blue, yet suddenly I saw one, and the sight gladdened my fading spirit. Kingfishers fly so quickly that by the time one says 'Look!', they have gone.

This most brilliant metallic bird is said to have such an unpleasant smell for other birds that it is solitary and safe. Then I visited the haunt, a tree by the river, and one day not only did a kingfisher fly past me but it landed on some reeds by the river's edge. Here it stayed a while, then was joined by another one. I am hoping that a family will be hatched in the spring and that they will always stay in the water-garden.

CECIL BEATON

KITCHEN GARDENS

Ever since I read Beatrix Potter's charming Peter Rabbit stories I've had a romantic view of kitchen gardens. There is something timeless and reassuring about the idea of an efficiently run kitchen garden providing an abundance of delicous fresh produce for the big house. Of course there has to be a skilful, if slightly dour, gardener in the mould of Mr MacGregor, the scourge of rabbits everywhere, and the sort of man who, in the idealized world of drawing-room comedies, arrives at the kitchen door with an old-fashioned trug full of good things which he deposits on the scrubbed deal table with a grunt, being a man of few words. Cook, also well scrubbed, then gives him a cup of tea and a slice of her scrumptious plum cake. He tucks in, grunts his thanks, and returns to the scene of his unceasingly productive labours, a man at one with nature and at peace with his soul. Such are the romantic notions of a child brought up in the more restricted world of suburbia.

My kitchen has likewise its particular quarters assigned to it; for besides the wholesome luxury which that place abounds with, I have always thought a kitchen-garden a more pleasant sight than the finest orangery, or artificial green-house. I love to see every thing in its perfection; and am more pleased to survey my rows of coleworts and cabbages, with a thousand nameless pot-herbs, springing up in their full fragrancy and verdure, than to see the tender plants of foreign countries kept alive by artificial heats, or withering in the air and soil that are not adapted to them.

JOSEPH ADDISON *The Spectator*

If well managed, nothing is more beautiful than the kitchen garden:
the earliest blossoms come there: we shall in vain seek for flowering
shrubs in March, and early in April, to equal the peaches, nectarines,
apricots, and plums; late in April, we shall find nothing to equal the
pear and the cherry; and, in May, the dwarf, or espalier, apple-trees,
are just so many immense garlands of carnations. The walks are
unshaded: they are not greasy or covered with moss, in the spring of
the year, like those in the shrubberies: to watch the progress of crops
is by no means unentertaining to any rational creature; and the
kitchen-garden gives you all this long before the ornamental part of
the garden affords you any thing worth looking at.

WILLIAM COBBETT *The English Gardener*
1829

No parterres, no fountains, no statues, embellished this little garden.
Its only ornament was a short walk, shaded on each side by a filbert-
hedge, with a small alcove at one end, whither in hot weather the
gentleman and his wife used to retire and divert themselves with
their children, who played in the walk before them. But, though
vanity had no votary in this little spot, here was a variety of fruit and
everything useful for the kitchen, which was abundantly sufficient to
catch the admiration of Adams, who told the gentleman he had
certainly a good gardener. Sir, answered he, that gardener is now
before you; whatever you see here is the work solely of my own
hands. Whilst I am providing necessaries for my table, I likewise
procure myself an appetite for them

HENRY FIELDING *Joseph Andrews*

LANDSCAPE GARDENERS

This witty piece is by A A Milne who is, of course, best known for his wonderful stories about Christopher Robin and Winnie-the-Pooh. The fame these immortal stories for children has brought him has obscured the fact that he was a regular contributor to *Punch* and between the wars he was one of Britain's most successful playwrights. He specialized in light comedies such as *Mr Pim Passes By*. Sadly these have been rather out of fashion recently but one play he wrote is a great favourite of mine. It is *Toad of Toad Hall*, which he adapted from Kenneth Grahame's *The Wind in the Willows*. Hardly a Christmas goes by without this super little classic bringing delight to children somewhere.

Really I know nothing about flowers. By a bit of luck, James, my gardener, whom I pay half a crown a week for combing the beds, knows nothing about them either; so my ignorance remains undiscovered. But in other people's gardens I have to make something of an effort to keep up appearances. Without flattering myself I may say that I have acquired a certain manner; I give the impression of the garden lover, or the man with shares in a seed company, or — or something.

For instance, at Creek Cottage, Mrs Atherley will say to me, 'That's an *Amphilobertus Gemini*,' pointing to something which I hadn't noticed behind a rake.

'I am not a bit surprised,' I say calmly.

'And a *Gladiophinium Banksii* next to it.'

'I suspected it,' I confess in a hoarse whisper.

Towards flowers whose names I know I adopt a different tone.

'Aren't you surprised to see daffodils out so early?' says Mrs Atherley with pride.

'There are lots out in London,' I mention casually. 'In the shops.'

'So there are grapes,' says Miss Atherley.

'I was not talking about grapes,' I reply stiffly.

However, at Creek Cottage just now I can afford to be natural; for it is not gardening which comes under discussion these days, but landscape-gardening, and any one can be an authority on that. The Atherleys, fired by my tales of Sandringham, Chatsworth, Arundel, and other places where I am constantly spending the week-end, are readjusting their two-acre field. In future it will not be called 'the garden,' but 'the grounds.'

I was privileged to be shown over the grounds on my last visit to Creek Cottage.

'Here,' said Mrs Atherley, 'we are having a plantation. It will keep the wind off; and we shall often sit here in the early days of summer. That's a weeping ash in the middle. There's another one over there. They'll be lovely, you know.'

'What's that?' I asked, pointing to a bit of black stick on the left; which, even more than the other trees, gave the impression of having been left there by the gardener while he went for his lunch.

'That's a weeping willow.'

'This is rather a tearful corner of the grounds,' apologized Miss Atherley. 'We'll show you something brighter directly. Look there — that's the oak in which King Charles lay hid. At least, it will be when it's grown a bit.'

'Let's go on to the shrubbery,' said Mrs Atherley. 'We are having a new grass path from here to the shrubbery. It's going to be called Henry's Walk.'

Miss Atherley has a small brother called Henry. Also there were eight Kings of England called Henry. Many a time and oft one of those nine Henrys has paced up and down this grassy walk, his head bent, his hands clasped behind his back; while behind his furrowed brow, who shall say what world-schemes were hatching? Is it the thought of Wolsey which makes him frown — or is he wondering where he left his catapult? Ah! who can tell us? Let us leave a veil of mystery over it . . . for the sake of the next visitor.

'The shrubbery,' said Mrs Atherley proudly, waving her hand at a couple of laurel bushes and a — I've forgotten its name now, but it is one of the few shrubs I really know.

'And if you're a gentleman,' said Miss Atherley, 'and want to get asked here again, you'll always *call* it the shrubbery.'

'Really, I don't see what else you could call it,' I said, wishing to be asked down again.

'The patch.'

'True,' I said.

'I mean, Nonsense.'

I was rather late for
breakfast next
morning; a pity
on such a
lovely spring day.

'I'm so sorry,' I began, 'but I was looking at the shrubbery from my window and I quite forgot the time.'

'Good,' said Miss Atherley.

'I must thank you for putting me in such a perfect room for it,' I went on, warming to my subject. 'One can actually see the shrubs — er — shrubbing. The plantation, too, seems a little thicker to me than yesterday.'

'I expect it is.'

'In fact, the tennis lawn——' I looked round anxiously. I had a sudden fear that it might be the new deer-park. 'It still is the tennis lawn?' I asked.

'Yes. Why, what about it?'

'I was only going to say the tennis lawn had quite a lot of shadows on it. Oh, there's no doubt that the plantation is really asserting itself.'

Eleven o'clock found me strolling in the grounds with Miss Atherley.

'You know,' I said, as we paced Henry's Walk together, 'the one thing the plantation wants is for a bird to nest in it. That is the hall-mark of a plantation.'

'It's mother's birthday to-morrow. Wouldn't it be a lovely surprise for her?'

'It would, indeed. Unfortunately this is a matter in which you require the co-operation of a feathered friend.'

'Couldn't you try to persuade a bird to build a nest in the weeping ash? Just for this once?'

'You're asking me a very difficult thing,' I said doubtfully. 'Anything else I would do cheerfully for you; but to dictate to a bird on such a very domestic affair — No, I'm afraid I must refuse.'

'It need only just *begin* to build one,' pleaded Miss Atherley, 'because mother's going up to town by your train to-morrow. As soon as she's out of the house the bird can go back anywhere else it likes better.'

'I will put that to any bird I see to-day,' I said, 'but I am doubtful.'

'Oh, well,' sighed Miss Atherley, 'never mind.'

'What do you think?' cried Mrs Atherley as she came in to breakfast next day. 'There's a bird been nesting in the plantation!'

Miss Atherley looked at me in undisguised admiration. I looked quite surprised — I know I did.

'Well, well!' I said.

'You must come out afterwards and see the nest and tell me what bird it is. There are three eggs in it. I am afraid I don't know much about these things.'

'I'm glad,' I said thankfully. 'I mean, I shall be glad to.'

We went out eagerly after breakfast. On about the only tree in the plantation with a fork to it a nest balanced precariously. It had in it three pale-blue eggs splotched with light brown. It appeared to be a blackbird's nest with another egg or two to come.

'It's been very quick about it,' said Miss Atherley.

'Of our feathered bipeds,' I said, frowning at her, 'the blackbird is notoriously the most hasty.'

'Isn't it lovely?' said Mrs Atherley.

She was still talking about it as she climbed into the trap which was to take us to the station.

'One moment,' I said, 'I've forgotten something.' I dashed into the house and out by a side door, and then sprinted for the plantation. I took the nest from the weeping and over-weighted ash and put it carefully back in the hedge by the tennis-lawn. Then I returned more leisurely to the house.

If you ever want a job of landscape-gardening thoroughly well done, you can always rely upon me.

A A MILNE
1914

LAWNS

Now I have a motorized mower I can agree with a certain amount of complacency that a lawn like the surface of a billiard table should be the aspiration of every British gardener who has more space than a window box. If I still relied on a hand mower I think I would have given in to the temptation of astroturf long ago. Well perhaps not, but I should certainly spend a lot of the summer grumbling. I once received some rather ingenious advice on the subject of lawns. 'Add a little brandy to your watering can,' counselled a gardening friend. 'That way you can be sure your lawn will come up half-cut!'

A PERFECT LAWN

The glory of the Small House at Allington certainly consists in its lawn, which is as smooth, as level, and as much like velvet as grass has ever yet been made to look. Lily Dale, taking pride in her own lawn, has declared often that it is no good attempting to play croquet up at the Great House. The grass, she says, grows in tufts, and nothing that Hopkins, the gardener, can or will do has any effect upon the tufts. But there are no tufts at the Small House. As the squire himself has never been very enthusiastic about croquet, the croquet implements have been moved permanently down to the Small House, and croquet there has become quite an institution.

And while I am on the subject of the garden I may also mention Mrs Dale's conservatory, as to which Bell was strenuously of

opinion that the Great House had nothing to offer equal to it —
'For flowers, of course, I mean,' she would say, correcting herself;
for at the Great House there was a grapery very celebrated. On this
matter the squire would be less tolerant than as regarded the
croquet, and would tell his niece that she knew nothing about
flowers. 'Perhaps not, Uncle Christopher,' she would say. 'All the
same, I like our geraniums best;' for there was a spice of obstinacy
about Miss Dale, — as, indeed, there was in all the Dales, male and
female, young and old.

ANTHONY TROLLOPE *The Small House at Allington*
1864

4 June 1889 Windsor

Its a glorious day, but rather too hot for Grandmama's & my taste,
so walking is an impossibility. Grandmama wrote in the garden this
morning & I sat not far off to be in readiness, lest she might want
anything. The flowers & grass smell so sweet, the whole is perfumed
& the birds sing beautifully as if their little throats were going to
burst. My rooms are splendid & the look-out from them is perfect.
Those grand old trees with their splendid foliage & the thick green
grass underneath is a sight to see — no one knows what grass is until
they come to England!

PRINCESS VICTORIA OF PRUSSIA,
granddaughter of Queen Victoria, to her mother,
DOWAGER EMPRESS FREDERICK OF PRUSSIA

MOWING IN THE GOOD OLD DAYS

The mowing was of course done by a stout pony in leather boots and the soothing hum of the mowing machine was one of the pleasures of summer, instead of the noisy, smelly mowers which one now has to endure.

AUDREY HOLLAND-HIBBERT *Hortus*

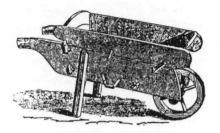

I love this moment from *David Copperfield*. It sums up the fierce proprietorial instinct which every gardener has about his or her patch of territory. I've seen people react in the same way at the sight of a neighbour's cat. Hell hath no fury like a gardener threatened.

DONKEYS!

Janet had gone away to get the bath ready, when my aunt, to my great alarm, became in one moment rigid with indignation, and had hardly voice to cry out, 'Janet! Donkeys!'

Upon which, Janet came running up the stairs as if the house were in flames, darted out on a little piece of green in front, and warned off two saddle-donkeys, lady-ridden, that had presumed to set hoof upon it; while my aunt, rushing out of the house, seized the bridle of a third animal laden with a bestriding child, turned him, led him forth from those sacred precincts, and boxed the ears of the unlucky urchin in attendance who had dared to profane that hallowed ground.

To this hour I don't know whether my aunt had any lawful right of way over that patch of green; but she had settled it in her own mind that she had, and it was all the same to her. The one great outrage of her life, demanding to be constantly avenged, was the passage of a donkey over that immaculate spot. In whatever occupation she was engaged, however interesting to her the conversation in which she was taking part, a donkey turned the current of her ideas in a moment, and she was upon him straight. Jugs of water, and watering-pots, were kept in secret places ready to be discharged on the offending boys; sticks were laid in ambush behind the door; sallies were made at all hours; and incessant war prevailed. Perhaps this was an agreeable excitement to the donkey-boys; or perhaps the more sagacious of the donkeys, understanding how the case stood, delighted with constitutional obstinacy in coming that way. I only know that there were three alarms before the bath was ready; and that on the occasion of the last and most desperate of all, I saw my aunt engage, single-handed, with a sandy-headed lad of fifteen, and bump his sandy head against her own gate, before he seemed to comprehend what was the matter.

CHARLES DICKENS *David Copperfield*
1850

LEEKS

The leek is a delicious vegetable and well worth finding space for if you have a vegetable plot. I don't think I have any Welsh blood to account for my fondness for leeks but I was reminded of the importance of the leek (not the more attractive but less authentic daffodil) as a Welsh emblem when I was playing Bardolph in Kenneth Branagh's film version of Shakespeare's *Henry V*. With his friends Nym and Pistol Bardolph is one of the ruffians who join Henry's army in France. Fluellen is a salt of the earth, non-commissioned officer and very Welsh indeed. When Fluellen is mocked by Pistol for wearing a leek in his cap – 'I am qualmish at the smell of leek' – Fluellen (brilliantly played by Ian Holm) forces him to eat an entire raw leek. And serve him right!

On one of my forays into secondhand book shops, I came across a fascinating book called *The Cook and Housewife's Manual* published in 1826. It is supposed to be by Megs Dod, who I believe is a character in one of Sir Walter Scott's novels. In fact it is by a Mrs Johnstone, the Scottish equivalent of Mrs Beeton, a hard-working journalist who could turn her hand to any topic. I have included the thoughts of both these excellent women on the subject of leeks.

The leek is one of the most honourable and ancient of pot-herbs. It is called *par excellence* the herb; and learned critics assert that our word porridge or pottage is derived from the Latin *porrus*, a *leek*. 'From Indus to Peru', the adoration of the garlic, onion, and leek is universal. The leek is the badge of a high-spirited, honourable, and fiery nation – the Ancient Britons. In the old poetry of the northern nations, where a young man would now be styled the *flower*, he was called 'the *leek* of his family, or tribe', an epithet of most savoury meaning.

Megs Dod
1826

THE LEEK

As in the case of the cucumber, this vegetable was bewailed by the Israelites in their journey through the desert. It is one of the alliaceous tribe, which consists of the onion, garlic, chive, shallot, and leek. These, as articles of food, are perhaps more widely diffused over the face of the earth than any other *genus* of edible plants. It is the national badge of the Welsh, and tradition ascribes its introduction to that part of Britain, to St David. The origin of the wearing of the leek on St David's day, among that people, is thus given in 'BEETON'S DICTIONARY OF UNIVERSAL INFORMATION:' — 'It probably originated from the custom of *Cymhortha*, or the friendly aid, practised among farmers. In some districts of South Wales, all the neighbours of a small farmer were wont to appoint a day when they attended to plough his land, and the like; and, at such time, it was the custom for each to bring his portion of leeks with him for making the broth or soup.' (See ST. DAVID.) Others derive the origin of the custom from the battle of Cressy. The plant, when grown in Wales and Scotland, is sharper than it is in England, and its flavour is preferred by many to that of the onion in broth. It is very wholesome, and, to prevent its tainting the breath, should be well boiled.

MRS BEETON
1861

Cock-a-leekie was largely consumed at the Burns Centenary Festival at the Crystal Palace, Sydenham, in 1859.

MRS BEETON
1861

LILACS

An elderly neighbour of ours used to warn us against bringing lilac into the house as she said it would herald a death. That seems a bit macabre to me and I must say I've never found it to be true. The smell of a lilac tree in full flower is one of life's great experiences. In fact the only fault I can find with lilac is having to get on a ladder to trim off all the finished flowers. This simple poem by Walt Whitman is a delight.

WHEN LILACS LAST IN THE DOORYARD BLOOM'D

In the dooryard fronting an old farm-house near the white-wash'd
    palings,
Stands the lilac-bush tall-growing with heart-shaped leaves of rich
    green,
With many a pointed blossom rising delicate, with the perfume
    strong I love,
With every leaf a miracle — and from this bush in the dooryard,
With delicate-color'd blossoms and heart-shaped leaves of rich
    green,
A sprig with its flower I break.

WALT WHITMAN

MANURE

Not a very savoury subject but one which has to find its place in any gardening anthology. A well manured garden repays dividends. All the same I prefer not to think about what has actually gone into the making of all those tasty homegrown vegetables. Suffice it to say 'Isn't nature wonderful?'

HOW TO FERTILISE SOIL

Of composts shall the Muse descend to sing,
Nor soil her heavenly plumes? The sacred Muse
Nought sordid deems, but what is base; nought fair
Unless true Virtue stamp it with her seal.
Then, planter, wouldst thou double thine estate;
Never, ah never, be asham'd to tread
Thy dung-heaps, where the refuse of thy mills,
With all the ashes, all thy coppers yield,
With weeds, mould, dung, and stale, a compost form,
Of force to fertilise the poorest soil.

JAMES GRAINGER
1721–66

         . . . The gardener
Should with rich mould or asses' solid dung
Or other ordure glut the starving earth
Bearing full baskets straining with the weight,
Nor should he hesitate to bring as food
For new ploughed fallow ground whatever stuff
The privy vomits from its filthy sewers.

COLUMELLA *De Re Rustica*
c 60 BC

To cherrish an Apple Tree: Throw al about your apple trees on the rootes thereof, the urine of old men, or of stale pisse long kept, they shall bring fruite much better . . .

LEONARD MASCALL *A Booke of the Arte and Maner howe to plant and graffe all sortes of trees. . .*
1572

The soil is a wonderful thing. . . . Treat it like a good old friend . . . give it the sort of nourishment it really appreciates . . . keep it in good heart — and it will reward you by growing almost anything your heart desires.

FRED STREETER

MAZES

Jerome K Jerome is a bit of a hero of mine. An effortlessly witty writer he was stage struck and tried his hand at being an actor for the very best of reasons 'I thought all acting was making love in tights to pretty women, and I determined to devote my life to it.'

His reflections on the experience still ring a bell with any Equity member, 'I can speak with authority on the subject of being hard up. I have been a provincial actor.'

He did not succeed as an actor but made a lot of money as a writer and wrote one of the minor classics of Eng Lit, *Three Men in a Boat*. In the eighteenth century, a maze became an essential ingredient of a well designed park and garden. Today there seems to be something of a maze revival. I'm all for it – I think gardens should be fun. Jerome K Jerome's account of how the three men get out of their boat for a visit to the maze at Hampton Court always reduces me to fits of laughter.

THREE MEN IN A MAZE

Harris asked me if I'd ever been in the maze at Hampton Court. He said he went in once to show somebody else the way. He had studied it up in a map, and it was so simple that it seemed foolish – hardly worth the twopence charged for admission. Harris said he thought that map must have been got up as a practical joke, because it wasn't a bit like the real thing, and only misleading. It was a country cousin that Harris took in. He said:

'We'll just go in here, so that you can say you've been, but it's very simple. It's absurd to call it a maze. You keep on taking the first turning to the right. We'll just walk round for ten minutes, and then go and get some lunch.'

They met some people soon after they had got inside, who said they had been there for three-quarters of an hour, and had had about enough of it. Harris told them they could follow him, if they liked; he was just going in, and then should turn round and come out again. They said it was very kind of him, and fell behind, and followed.

They picked up various other people who wanted to get it over, as they went along, until they had absorbed all the persons in the maze. People who had given up all hopes of ever either getting in or out, or of ever seeing their home and friends again, plucked up courage at the sight of Harris and his party, and joined the procession, blessing him. Harris said he should judge there must have been twenty people, following him, in all; and one woman with a baby, who had been there all the morning, insisted on taking his arm, for fear of losing him.

Harris kept on turning to the right, but it seemed a long way, and his cousin said he supposed it was a very big maze.

'Oh, one of the largest in Europe,' said Harris.

'Yes, it must be,' replied the cousin, 'because we've walked a good two miles already.'

Harris began to think it rather strange himself, but he held on until, at last, they passed the half of a penny bun on the ground that Harris's cousin swore he had noticed there seven minutes ago. Harris said: 'Oh, impossible!' but the woman with the baby said, 'Not at all,' as she herself had taken it from the child, and thrown it down there, just before she met Harris. She also added that she wished she never had met Harris, and expressed an opinion that he was an impostor. That made Harris mad, and he produced his map, and explained his theory.

'The map may be all right enough,' said one of the party, 'if you know whereabouts in it we are now.'

Harris didn't know, and suggested that the best thing to do would be to go back to the entrance, and begin again. For the beginning again part of it there was not much enthusiasm; but with regard to the advisability of going back to the entrance there was complete unanimity, and so they turned, and trailed after Harris again, in the opposite direction. About ten minutes more passed, and then they found themselves in the centre.

Harris thought at first of pretending that that was what he had been aiming at; but the crowd looked dangerous, and he decided to treat it as an accident.

Anyhow, they had got something to start from then. They did know where they were, and the map was once more consulted, and the thing seemed simpler than ever, and off they started for the third time.

And three minutes later they were back in the centre again.

After that, they simply couldn't get anywhere else. Whatever way they turned brought them back to the middle. It became so regular at length that some of the people stopped there, and waited for the others to take a walk round, and come back to them. Harris drew out his map again, after a while, but the sight of it only infuriated the mob, and they told him to go and curl his hair with it. Harris said that he couldn't help feeling that, to a certain extent, he had become unpopular.

They all got crazy at last, and sang out for the keeper, and the man came and climbed up the ladder outside, and shouted out directions to them. But all their heads were, by this time, in such a confused whirl that they were incapable of grasping anything, and so the man told them to stop where they were, and he would come to them. They huddled together, and waited; and he climbed down, and came in.

He was a young keeper, as luck would have it, and new to the business; and when he got in, he couldn't find them, and he wandered about, trying to get to them, and then *he* got lost. They caught sight of him, every now and then, rushing about the other side of the hedge, and he would see them, and rush to get to them, and they would wait there for about five minutes, and then he would reappear again in exactly the same spot, and ask them where they had been.

They had to wait till one of the old keepers came back from his dinner before they got out.

Harris said he thought it was a very fine maze, so far as he was a judge; and we agreed that we would try to get George to go into it, on our way back.

JEROME K JEROME
1889

MEMORIES

No need to press the point that the garden you knew as a child stays with you for the rest of your life. Here are a few of my favourite garden memories.

THE GREY-WALLED GARDEN

There is a grey-walled garden far away
From noise and smoke of cities where the hours
Pass with soft wings among the happy flowers
And lovely leisure blossoms every day.

There, tall and white, the sceptral lily blows;
There grow the pansy pink and columbine,
Brave holly-hocks and star-white jessamine
And the red glory of the royal rose.

There greeny glow-worms gem the dusky lawn,
The lime-trees breathe their fragrance to the night,
Pink roses sleep, and dream that they are white
Until they wake to colour with the dawn.

There in the splendour of the sultry noon
The sunshine sleeps upon the garden bed,
Where the white poppy droops a drowsy head
And dreams of kisses from the white full moon.

*   *   *

And there, all day, my heart goes wandering,
Because there first my heart began to know
The glories of the summer and the snow,
The loveliness of harvest and of spring.

There may be fairer gardens – but I know
There is no other garden half so dear
Because 'tis there, this many, many a year,
The sacred sweet white flowers of memory grow.

E NESBIT

Now I am in the garden at the back ... – a very preserve of butterflies, as I remember it, with a high fence and a gate and padlock; where the fruit clusters on the trees, riper and richer than fruit has ever been since, in any other garden, and where my mother gathers some in a basket, while I stand by, bolting furtive gooseberries, and trying to look unmoved.

CHARLES DICKENS *David Copperfield*
1850

THE GARDEN AT LA HAYE

Two great brown gates swung back on their hinges and we passed through them into the courtyard of the dearest home of my childhood. The courtyard was square. One side was formed by the house; dairy, coach-house and the chicken-house formed the second side; on the third were stable, cow-houses and goat-shed; on the fourth wood-shed, dog-kennel and the great gates by which we had entered. The house itself was an ordinary white-washed, slate-roofed, French country house, with an immense walled fruit garden on the other side of it.

There never was such another garden, there never will be! Peaches, apricots, nectarines, and grapes of all kinds, lined the inside walls; the avenue that ran down the middle of it was of fig trees and standard peach-trees. There were raspberries, cherries and straw-berries, and flowers mingling with fruits and vegetables in a confusion the most charming in the world. Along the end of the garden was a great arcade of black, clipped yews, so thick and strong that a child could crawl on the outside of it without falling through. Above the dairy and coach-house was an immense hay-loft, a straw-loft over the stable and cow-house. What play-rooms for wet days! Beyond the chicken-house was the orchard full of twisted grey apple trees, beneath whose boughs in due season the barley grew. Beyond, a network of lanes, fringed with maiden-hair, led away into fairyland.

My brothers eagerly led me round to show me all the treasures of the new home. There was a swing in the orchard, there were trees full of cherries, white and black.

'And we may eat as many as we like,' said Alfred.

That afternoon we gathered a waste-paper basket full of cherries, and, with strenuous greed, set ourselves to empty it. We didn't succeed, of course, but the effort, so far as I remember, was attended by no evil consequences. We gave what we couldn't eat to the little black English pig, another of the treasures of the new home.

E Nesbit

THE GARDEN OF THE STRAWBERRY-PINK VILLA

This doll's-house garden was a magic land, a forest of flowers through which roamed creatures I had never seen before. Among the thick, silky petals of each rose-bloom lived tiny, crab-like spiders that scuttled sideways when disturbed. Their small, translucent bodies were coloured to match the flowers they inhabited: pink, ivory, wine-red, or buttery-yellow. On the rose-stems, encrusted with green flies, lady-birds moved like newly painted toys; lady-birds pale red with large black spots; lady-birds apple-red with brown spots; lady-birds orange with grey-and-black freckles. Rotund and amiable, they prowled and fed among the anaemic flocks of greenfly. Carpenter bees, like furry, electric-blue bears, zigzagged among the flowers, growling fatly and busily. Humming-bird hawk-moths, sleek and neat, whipped up and down the paths with a fussy efficiency, pausing occasionally on speed-misty wings to lower a long, slender proboscis into a bloom. Among the white cobbles large black ants staggered and gesticulated in groups round strange trophies: a dead caterpillar, a piece of rose-petal, or dried grass-head fat with seeds. As an accompaniment to all this activity there came from the olive-groves outside the fuchsia hedge the incessant shimmering cries of the cicadas. If the curious, blurring heat-haze produced a sound, it would be exactly the strange, chiming cries of these insects.

Gerald Durrell *My Family and Other Animals*

MISTLETOE MAGIC

By sitting uppon a hill late in an evening, neere a wood, in a fewe nights a firedrake (Will o' the wisp) will appear; marke where it lighteth, and there you shall find an oake with Mistletoe therein, at the roote wherof there is a misselchild, whereof many strange things are conceived.

HUGH PLAT
1608

MOONLIGHT

The moonbeams fell upon the roof and garden of Gerrard. It suffused the cottage with its brilliant light, except where the dark depth of the embowered porch defied its entry. All round the beds of flowers and herbs spread sparkling and defined. You could trace the minutest walk; almost distinguish every leaf. Now and then there came a breath, and the sweet-peas murmured in their sleep or the roses rustled, as if they were afraid they were about to be roused from their lightsome dreams. Farther on the fruit trees caught the splendour of the night; and looked like a troop of sultanas taking their garden air, when the eye of man could not prophane them, and laden with jewels. There were apples that rivalled rubies; pears of topaz tint; a whole paraphernalia of plums, some purple as the amethyst, others blue and brilliant as the sapphire; an emerald here, and now a golden drop that gleamed like the yellow diamond of Gengis Khan.

BENJAMIN DISRAELI *Sybil*
1845

NEWSPAPERS

FRED STREETER ON GARDENING WITH NEWSPAPERS

'I've shown you that cauliflowers have a sweet tooth. But did you know that runner beans love a diet of newspapers?'

Fred knew full well that remarks like these were sure-fire conversation stoppers; he loved to hear how listeners would be halted in the middle of their cornflake breakfasts or transfixed in the course of shaving the moment he produced his latest improbable comment on the air!

'Don't get me wrong,' he would continue, 'it's not that those runner beans can *read*. It's simply that they make the perfect lining for your bean trench before you top it up with compost and soil. The newspapers hold moisture splendidly, so even if we get a long, dry spell, the moisture from the rotting paper will steadily seep into the growing roots and help to keep them fit and healthy.'

Having heard this explanation, no doubt I looked suitably impressed because old Fred gave me a knowing wink and added – 'Of course, if you like your beans with plenty of sauce, you'd better give them those cheeky newspapers with one or two pin-ups. That should keep them happy down there in the trench!'

FRANK HENNING *Cheerio Frank, Cheerio Everybody*

ONE-UPMANSHIP IN THE GARDEN

No good pretending that all gardeners are motivated by the purest motives all the time. For every ten generous souls who distribute cuttings in a spirit of gardening camaraderie there is someone who sees gardening as just another opportunity for getting one up. To digress for a moment on the subject of cuttings, I love the story about the vicar visiting a famous garden who, despite the teachings of the church, couldn't control the urge to cut little bits off the many exotic plants. Unfortunately, coming across the lady of the house, instinctive politeness forced him to raise his panama and he was showered with cuttings.

E F Benson, himself the son of an Archbishop of Canterbury, catches perfectly the world of the small country town in his books about Riseholme, with its vicars, retired colonels, ladies of the manor and those two energetic social climbers, Miss Mapp and 'Lucia' Lucas. The following is a classic example of gardening one-upmanship.

Miss Mapp had found such difficulty in getting eight players together to-day, that she had transgressed her principles and asked Mrs Poppit as well as Isabel, and they, with Diva, the two Bartletts, and the Major and the Captain, formed the party. The moment Mrs Poppit appeared, Elizabeth hated her more than ever, for she put up her glasses, and began to give her patronizing advice about her garden, which she had not been allowed to see before.

'You have quite a pretty little piece of garden, Miss Mapp,' she said, 'though, to be sure, I fancied from what you said that it was more extensive. Dear me, your roses do not seem to be doing very well. Probably they are old plants and want renewing. You must send your gardener round – you keep a gardener? – and I will let you have a dozen vigorous young bushes.'

Miss Mapp licked her dry lips. She kept a kind of gardener: two days a week.

'Too good of you,' she said, 'but that rose-bed is quite sacred, dear Mrs Poppit. Not all the vigorous young bushes in the world would tempt me. It's my "Friendship's Border": some dear friend gave me each of my rose-trees.'

Mrs Poppit transferred her gaze to the wistaria that grew over the steps up to the garden-room. Some of the dear friends she thought must be centenarians.

'Your wistaria wants pruning sadly,' she said. 'Your gardener does not understand wistarias. That corner there was made, I may say, for fuchsias. You should get a dozen choice fuchsias.'

Miss Mapp laughed.

'Oh, you must excuse me,' she said with a glance at Mrs Poppit's brocaded silk. 'I can't bear fuchsias. They always remind me of over-dressed women.'

E F BENSON *Miss Mapp*
1922

ONIONS AND GARLIC

THE ONION

Like the cabbage, this plant was erected into an object of worship by the idolatrous Egyptians 2,000 years before the Christian era, and it still forms a favourite food in the country of these people, as well as in other parts of Africa. When it was first introduced to England, has not been ascertained; but it has long been in use, and esteemed as a favourite seasoning plant to various dishes. In warmer climates it is much milder in its flavour; and such as are grown in Spain and Portugal, are, comparatively speaking, very large, and are often eaten both in a boiled and roasted state. The Strasburg is the most esteemed; and, although all the species have highly nutritive properties, they impart such a disagreeable odour to the breath, that they are often rejected even where they are liked. Chewing a little raw parsley is said to remove this odour.

Mrs Beeton
1861

OF ONIONS, GARLIC AND SOCIAL UNITY

I know that there is supposed to be a prejudice against the onion; but I think there is rather a cowardice in regard to it. I doubt not that all men and women love the onion; but few confess their love. Affection for it is concealed. Good New-Englanders are as shy of owning it as they are of talking about religion. Some people have days on which they eat onions,—what you might call 'retreats,' or their 'Thursdays.' The act is in the nature of a religious ceremony, an Eleusinian mystery; not a breath of it must get abroad. On that day they see no company; they deny the kiss of greeting to the dearest friend; they retire within themselves, and hold communion with one of the most pungent and penetrating manifestations of the moral vegetable world. Happy is said to be the family which can eat onions together. They are, for the time being, separate from the world, and have a harmony of aspiration. There is a hint here for the reformers. Let them become apostles of the onion; let them eat, and preach it to their fellows, and circulate tracts of it in the form of seeds. In the onion is the hope of universal brotherhood. If all men will eat onions at all times, they will come into a universal sympathy. . . .

Look at Italy . . . It is the food of the common people of Italy. All the social atmosphere of that delicious land is laden with it. Its odour is a practical democracy. In the churches all are alike: there is one faith, one smell. The entrance of Victor Emanuel into Rome is only the pompous proclamation of a unity which garlic had already accomplished; and yet we, who boast of our democracy, eat onions in secret.

CHARLES DUDLEY WARNER *Pusley*
1880

Annie and I are very keen on homemade soup so I thought I'd share the Briers' recipe for Onion Soup in this section. It's simple and delicious.

ANNIE'S FRENCH ONION SOUP

4 large onions, thinly sliced
1½ ozs butter or margarine
1 generous tablespoon sugar (brown is nice but you can use white)
2 pints vegetable or chicken stock
Dash of white wine or white wine vinegar
Salt and freshly ground black pepper

Melt the butter or margarine in a large frying pan and add the onions. Stir with a wooden spoon until they soften. Then add the sugar and continue to stir until the onions are a good brown (but not black!) colour. Transfer to a large saucepan. Add the stock and the white wine or wine vinegar. Simmer for about 20 minutes and season to taste with salt and pepper.

You can serve this plain, with toasted French bread floating on top or thickly sprinkled with grated cheese.

Serves 4.

PESTS AND
PARASITES

One often has the feeling of being entirely overwhelmed by pests, particularly the *tiny* ones. Having planted a small rose garden near an oak tree I had just got to grips with the green and black fly when I was stopped in my tracks by a group of small, white caterpillars calmly parachuting, or was it abseiling, down from the oak tree on to the roses below with the aid of thin silk threads. A terrible thought struck me. Caterpillars have *minds*. How can you cope with that!

Cats are ranked highly as garden pests by some people – *other* people's cats of course, not one's own darling Tiggy. A little cat pepper scattered around your prize exhibits may help to deter, but as we all know, a cat is a cat is a cat and will eventually do exactly what it wants, exactly *where* it wants.

I can't really bring myself to be beastly to moles since playing Ratty in *Wind in the Willows* a few years ago. Moley was such a dear old character, so houseproud and so fond of his garden, I feel real moles must be like that. Silly I know, but there it is. However, I am reliably informed that if you want your mole to move house you should scatter mothballs outside his front door, he really cannot abide the smell.

The worst ENEMYES to gardens are Moles, Catts, Earewiggs, Snailes and Mice, and they must be carefully destroyed, or all your labor all the year long is lost.

The Garden Book of Sir Thomas Hanmer
1653

GREEN FLY

Of every single garden pest,
I think I hate the Green Fly best.
My hate for him is stern and strong:
I've hated him both loud and long.
Since first I met him in the spring
I've hated him like anything.

There was one Green Fly, I recall:
I hated him the most of all.
He sat upon my finest rose,
And put his finger to his nose.
Then sneered, and turned away his head
To bite my rose of royal red.

Next day I noticed, with alarm,
That he had started out to charm
A lady fly, as green in hue
As all the grass that ever grew.
He wooed, he won; she named the night –
And gave my rose another bite.

Ye gods, quoth I, if this goes on,
Before another week has gone,
These two will propagate their kind
Until one morning I shall find
A million Green Fly on my roses,
All with their fingers to their noses.

I made a fire, I stoked it hot
With all the rubbish I had got;
I picked the rose of royal red
Which should have been their bridal bed;
And on the day they twain were mated
They also were incinerated.

REGINALD ARKELL

Greenfly, it's difficult to see
Why God, who made the rose, made thee.

A P HERBERT *Look Back and Laugh*
1890–1971

PARASITE'S PARADISE

The garden holds the high, still peace of summer.
    All creatures hush; no bird-song, beetle-yell.
My deck-chair hushes; *I* could not be dumber.
    Emerald peace! And, underneath it—hell!

This sun-spread scene of woodland, lawn and orchard,
    This green Jerusalem, this Mon Repos —
The whole half-acre's being slowly tortured.
    (A rhyme designed to stimulate real woe.)

Look at the lily, dreaming on her lover,
    Drooping towards his wild embrace or hug!
Look. Very closely. What do you discover?
    The drooping's caused by some revolting bug.

The nodding rose, the pendulous carnation
    Wilt in the green-fly's nauseating grip.
Massed aphides of every coloration
    Are giving the herbaceous border gyp.

No noise! No rumour! But the broad-bean narrows,
    The drowsing pea is riddled by the worm,
Uncounted molars masticate the marrows
    And make the sleeping spinach fairly squirm.

Unheard, ten million mandibles are smacking,
    Five million silent mouths are bulged with shrubs;
The whole pleasaunce is getting a shellacking —
    Eden is being eaten by the grubs.

$$\star \qquad \star \qquad \star$$

This leads to very cosmic speculations —
    Is Peace no more than Hidden War, *e.g.*?
Is Man a parasite? Are ants relations?
    Then should one bump them off with D.D.T.?

Reader—if any—each is a dilemma
    Which normally would cause me grave distress;
However, this is Sunday *and* pip-emma,
    The sun is shining—I could *not* care less.

JUSTIN RICHARDSON *Punch*
July 1947

AN INVASION

As we have remarked that insects are often conveyed from one country to another in a very unaccountable manner, I shall here mention an emigration of small *Aphides*, which was observed in the village of Selborne no longer ago than August the 1st, 1785.

At about three o'clock in the afternoon of that day, which was very hot, the people of this village were surprised by a shower of *Aphides*, or smother-flies, which fell in these parts. Those that were walking in the street at that juncture found themselves covered with these insects, which settled also on the hedges and gardens, blackening all the vegetables where they lighted. My annuals were discoloured with them, and the stalks of a bed of onions were quite coated over for six days after. These armies were then, no doubt, in a state of emigration, and shifting their quarters; and might have come, as far as we know, from the great hop-plantations of Kent or Sussex, the wind being all that day in the easterly quarter. They were observed at the same time in great clouds about Farnham, and all along the vale from Farnham to Alton.

GILBERT WHITE *Natural History and Antiquities of Selborne*
1788

Sometimes we try to be a bit too clever in this world. Take the poor old gardener who's plagued by blackfly. He'll spend a small fortune on sprays and things when all he need do is take a little soil from the bottom of the plant and sprinkle it like powder all over those blessed blackfly. That'll finish them off . . . it gets in their teeth you know!

FRED STREETER

PEAS

We are all so spoiled these days. We've lost the pleasure and anticipation of vegetables in their proper season now that crates of out-of-season fruit and vegetables are air-freighted across continents to satisfy our insatiable demands. But maybe we've lost as much as we've gained. When you can have a thing all the time it is never as desirable as when you have to wait for it. Not that I have an axe to grind on the subject of frozen peas. It's just that I remember how delicous fresh peas were. My mother used to sit my sister and me outside the kitchen door with a great pile of peas, in real pods, and we would open them up and scrape them into a saucepan for what seemed like hours. But by golly they were good, raw or cooked, and the texture was quite different from the frozen variety. After a winter of cabbage, parsnip and swede we were delighted when the peas came into season.

I decided to see what Mrs Beeton had to say on the subject, before the advent of mass-produced frozen food. Of course she comes up trumps with lots of fascinating facts plus a recipe for pea and lettuce soup which is mouth watering. I have included Mrs B's original but I should point out that these days you will probably use a food blender, not a sieve. Also, for an average 4–5 servings you need to halve all the quantities. Even so you'll be hard put to do it for the same price.

THE PEA

It is supposed that the common gray pea, found wild in Greece, and other parts of the Levant, is the original of the common garden pea, and of all the domestic varieties belonging to it. The gray, or field pea, called *bisallie* by the French, is less subject to run into varieties than the garden kinds, and is considered by some, perhaps on that account, to be the wild plant, retaining still a large proportion of its original habit. From the tendency of all other varieties 'to run away' and become different to what they originally were, it is very difficult to determine the races to which they belong. The pea was well known to the Romans, and, probably, was introduced to Britain at an early period; for we find peas mentioned by Lydgate, a poet of the 15th century, as being hawked in London. They seem, however, for a considerable time, to have fallen out of use; for, in the reign of Queen Elizabeth, Fuller tells us they were brought from Holland, and were accounted 'fit dainties for ladies, they came so far and cost so dear.' There are some varieties of peas which have no lining in their pods, which are eaten cooked in the same way as kidney-beans. They are called *sugar* pease, and the best variety is the large crooked sugar, which is also very good, used in the common way, as a culinary vegetable. There is also a white sort, which readily splits when subjected to the action of millstones set wide apart, so as not to grind them. These are used largely for soups, and especially for sea-stores. From the quantity of farinaceous and saccharine matter contained in the pea, it is highly nutritious as an article of food.

PEA SOUP (GREEN)

INGREDIENTS.—3 pints of green peas, ¼ lb. of butter, 2 or three thin slices of ham, 6 onions sliced, 4 shredded lettuces, the crumb of 2 French rolls, 2 handfuls of spinach, 1 lump of sugar, 2 quarts of common stock.

Mode.—Put the butter, ham, 1 quart of the peas, onions, and lettuces, to a pint of stock, and simmer for an hour; then add the remainder of the stock, with the crumb of the French rolls, and boil for another hour. Now boil the spinach, and squeeze it very dry. Rub the soup through a sieve, and the spinach with it, to colour it. Have ready a pint of *young* peas boiled; add them to the soup, put in the sugar, give one boil, and serve. If necessary, add salt.

Time.—2½ hours. *Average cost*, 1*s*. 9*d*. per quart.

Seasonable from June to the end of August.

Sufficient for 10 persons.

Note.—It will be well to add, if the peas are not quite young, a little sugar. Where economy is essential, water may be used instead of stock for this soup, boiling in it likewise the pea-shells; but use a double quantity of vegetables.

MRS BEETON
1861

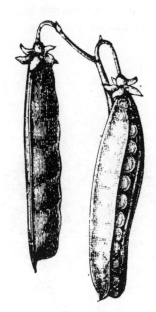

PSYCHOLOGY

Psychology is an important factor in gardening and caring for plants. We've all had plants that drooped in one situation and thrived merrily when moved somewhere else that was theoretically no more suitable. House plants like to huddle together. If left singly they do not do as well. I often practise my lines on plants. They like to know what I'm up to and they never mind how often I go over a speech.

My wife has an impressive collection of cacti and succulents which she insists on keeping in an upstairs bathroom. Now, not only are cacti a bit of a hazard in the bathroom, but not many people get to see them, which seems a shame as they really are rather splendid. I've tried everything to get her to move them downstairs, but she won't budge. 'They like it up there,' she insists, 'and I can talk to them while I am in the bath.' So there you have it – the power of plant psychology.

To get the best results you must talk to your vegetables.

PRINCE CHARLES

I hope at some future time to be allowed—even encouraged—to refer to such things as the most artistic way to frame cucumbers, how to stop tomatoes blushing (the homoeopathic method of putting them next to the French beans is now discredited), and spring fashions in fox gloves. But for the moment I have said enough. The great thing to remember in gardening is that flowers, fruits and vegetables alike can only be cultivated with sympathy. Special attention should be given to backward and delicate plants. They should be encouraged to make the most of themselves. Never forget that flowers, like ourselves, are particular about the company they keep. If a hyacinth droops in the celery bed, put it among the pansies.

A A Milne *Those Were the Days*
1929

If those who differ on speculative points should walk together now and then in the country, they might find many objects that must unite them.

Walter Landor

QUEEN VICTORIA AND QUEEN MARY

These two great ladies both had an important influence on royal gardens. Queen Victoria because of all that buying and building at Windsor, Osborne and Balmoral; Queen Mary because she was a keen gardener herself. The beautiful circular rose garden in Regent's Park is named after her. She was famous for her crusade against ivy, which she regarded as an unmitigated scourge. I love to think of her turning all the strength of her formidable personality on the hapless ivy. She dragooned friends and staff on to her 'Ivy Squad' and her hosts at various country houses lived in dread of her arrival.

DOWN WITH IVY

25 September 1939
Lovely morning which we spent clearing ivy off trees in the grounds while Jack Coke hacked off branches off 2 chestnut trees & an elm not far from the house & the gardeners began to clear a wall of ivy near Mary B's bedroom.

26 September 1939
Lovely morning which we spent clearing ivy off trees – We watched a whole wall of ivy of 50 years standing at the back of Mary B's bedroom being removed – most of it came down like a blanket.

QUEEN MARY *Diary entries while staying at Badminton*

QUEEN VICTORIA'S GARDENS AT FROGMORE, WINDSOR

The finest sight at Frogmore is undoubtedly the conservatories and glass-houses. They are practically without number, as additions are frequently made, and they form a veritable township. The loftiest among them is the Palm House, a really fine structure containing a most valuable collection of palms, ferns, and foliage plants. Next in size is the Conservatory, where are grown every year thousands of splendid camellias, gardenias, and azalea blooms. The camellias in particular are enormous plants.

The Queen's favourite houses are those devoted to the more delicate kind of roses. These she is very fond of visiting. An interminable quantity of glass is also given up to the cultivation of flowers and foliage of every kind. It is noticeable that Her Majesty has never yielded to the fashionable craze for orchids, and only a small house is given up to the cultivation of a few ordinary kinds at Frogmore. Two houses are, however, filled with the peculiar 'carnivorous' plants, which are as uncanny as they are curious, and which emit a most disagreeable odour.

The sight in these most wonderful Royal Gardens is the Pineries. There are eight pits of a total length of four hundred feet. On a hot morning when the pits are opened and each ripening pine sits like a crowned queen on her splendid throne of huge sword-edged grey-green leaves, the sight is most imposing, while the perfume can be scented half-way across the gardens. Pines for the Queen's table are grown of about eight pounds' weight, and are served to her all the year round.

Her Majesty has a fancy only to eat strawberries grown on the Frogmore estate, and wherever she may be, at home or abroad, strawberries are sent to her every day.

There being over two miles of wall at Frogmore it is easily understood that the quantity of outdoor fruit grown is immense. Two hundred and fifty varieties of pears alone are cultivated, and the same variety of apples. When fruit is grown under glass, as it ripens, each piece is carefully inclosed in a bag of white tissue paper to prevent wasps or flies from touching it.

And yet this immense garden—which is divided into eight portions, each under a foreman, who is again responsible to Mr Owen Thomas—is scarcely large enough to supply the Royal Household, and very often there are not enough potatoes produced by the twelve acres devoted to their growth to serve the Royal residences all the year round, and others have to be bought.

Besides the outdoor asparagus beds, which are in length two thousand two hundred and twenty yards, a great deal of this delicious vegetable is grown under glass; there are also five miles of peas. Of the fruit consumed in the Royal Household the return of one year gives a fair idea.

1,673 dozens of dessert apples,
1,500 dozens and 20 pecks of pears,
1,250lbs. of cherries,
5,150lbs. of grapes,
(to which the famous old vines at
Cumberland Lodge and Hampton
Court contribute)

520 dozen peaches,
239 pineapples,
400 melons,
2,700lbs. of strawberries,
2,000lbs. of currants,
1,900lbs. of gooseberries,
220 dozen nectarines,

besides quantities of plums, cooking fruit, damsons, and other things. Vegetables are, of course, in like proportion, so it is easy to understand that the hundred and thirty men employed are not idle.

The Queen and all the Royal Family are great consumers of fruit and vegetables, and believe in their wholesome properties. As with the superfluous farm produce, all the garden produce that is not required at the Castles, is given away among certain people on the Royal estate.

Her Majesty is very well informed on the subject of horticulture, and is, when at Windsor, a frequent visitor to her gardens.

In Mr Thomas' house, there is a charming room kept sacred to the Queen's use. It is at one end of the building and is entered direct from the wide main walk by a large French window which opens on to two shallow stone steps.

The wall-paper is blue with rings of gold on it. The furniture of oak with cane seats is very simple, a table fills the centre of the room, and a stuffed cockatoo gives a touch of colour. Here, facing a stone-circled fountain and pond, where some goldfish sport and a sweet-smelling Cape waterweed flourishes, Her Majesty will sit and watch her grand-children riding small bicycles up and down the broad path and swimming boats on the pond.

The vast daily orders of fruit, flowers, and vegetables required for the Castle consumption are received by Mr Thomas from the various departments every morning at a small wooden office which rather disfigures the beautiful old covered court just outside the door of the great kitchen. The Clerk of the Kitchen, the *chef*, and the Table Deckers whose business it is to arrange Her Majesty's board, all state to him what they want. Certain other servants are deputed to change the great plants and palms that stand in the Grand Corridor, while an entirely separate order is given for flowers wherewith to decorate Her Majesty's private apartments. Sometimes, by the Queen's special wishes, flowers are sought for among the woods and hedgerows. In the spring particularly, the Queen likes to see wild flowers in her rooms, and for days at a time bluebells and primroses will replace the rare roses and lilies that are grown at the cost of so much toil and money.

The Private Life of the Queen by One of Her Majesty's Servants
1897

QUEEN MARY AT PETWORTH

When King George V was convalescing from a near fatal illness at nearby Bognor, Queen Mary was a regular visitor to Petworth. She would be driven over to Petworth through villages with rural, rugged names like Eartham and Duncton and Funtington – delighting on the journey to see the noble company of elms and oaks and chestnuts that stood guard along the peaceful lanes of Sussex.

Arriving at Petworth, the Queen would walk quietly in the gardens with one of her ladies-in-waiting. It was on just such a visit that she happened to peep into a hothouse to find Fred Streeter intent on the task of spraying with soft water a newly flowering family of blooms – a task he would entrust to no one else. The Queen had heard already that Fred was particularly proud of his orchids and she was anxious to know how they were progressing. But more than that . . . she wanted to solve another little mystery.

'Is it really true,' she enquired of Fred, 'that you actually talk to your flowers?' She had heard it rumoured, but she could scarcely credit that it was so.

'Perfectly true ma'am,' Fred assured her. 'I talk to them just like I talk to any other friends. And if one of them looks a bit sorry for himself I simply say – "Come on old chap, cheer up. Shall I fetch you a drink?" It works wonders you know ma'am, because plants have feelings just like the rest of us.'

Fred turned at this point to show the Queen a batch of cuttings that were prospering near by.

'Now take those cuttings ma'am,' he continued, 'when I first put them into that rooting medium, they looked just like little lost souls. In fact I was afraid I was going to lose the lot. But I said to them one morning – "Do you remember who your father was . . . he was a fine great plant and I want you all to grow up nice and strong so you'll be a credit to him." And after that they rooted away splendidly and they've never looked back.'

The Queen nodded gravely. 'I must remember that,' she said.

FRANK HENNING *Cheerio Frank, Cheerio Everybody*

RHUBARB

A A Milne really hits the nail on the head when on the subject of rhubarb. Personally, I feel about it the way Barbara Cartland feels about bananas – such an uninteresting fruit. Or is it a fruit? As ever Mrs Beeton has the answer. . . .

RHUBARB

This is one of the most useful of all garden productions that are put into pies and puddings. It was comparatively little known till within the last twenty or thirty years, but it is now cultivated in almost every British garden. The part used is the footstalks of the leaves, which, peeled and cut into small pieces, are put into tarts, either mixed with apples or alone. When quite young, they are much better not peeled. Rhubarb comes in season when apples are going out. The common rhubarb is a native of Asia; the scarlet variety has the finest flavour. Turkey rhubarb, the well-known medicinal drug, is the root of a very elegant plant (*Rheum palmatum*), coming to greatest perfection in Tartary. For culinary purposes, all kinds of rhubarb are the better for being blanched.

RHUBARB TART

INGREDIENTS.—½ lb. of puff-paste, about 5 sticks of large rhubarb, ¼ lb. of moist sugar.

Mode.—Make a puff-crust; line the edges of a deep pie-dish with it, and wash, wipe, and cut the rhubarb into pieces about 1 inch long. Should it be old and tough, string it, that is to say, pare off the outside skin. Pile the fruit high in the dish as it shrinks very much in the cooking; put in the sugar, cover with crust, ornament the edges, and bake the tart in a well-heated oven from ½ to ¾ hour. If wanted very nice, brush it over with the white of an egg beaten to a stiff froth, then sprinkle on it some sifted sugar, and put it in the oven just to set the glaze: this should be done when the tart is nearly baked. A small quantity of lemon-juice, and a little of the peel minced, are by many persons considered an improvement to the flavour of rhubarb tart.

Time.—½ to ¾ hour. *Average cost, 9d.*
Sufficient for 4 or 5 persons.
Seasonable in spring.

MRS BEETON
1861

THE RHUBARB BORDER

gives me more trouble than all the rest of the garden. I started it a year ago with the idea of keeping the sun off the young carnations. It acted excellently, and the complexion of the flowers was improved tenfold. Then one day I discovered James busily engaged in pulling up the rhubarb.

'What are you doing?' I cried. 'Do you want the young carnations to go all brown?'

'I was going to send some in to the cook,' he grumbled.

'To the cook! What do you mean? Rhubarb isn't a vegetable.'

'No, it's a fruit.'

I looked at James anxiously. He had a large hat on, and the sun couldn't have got to the back of his neck.

'My dear James,' I said, 'I don't pay you half a crown a week for being funny. Perhaps we had better make it two shillings in future.'

However, he persisted in his theory that in the spring people stewed rhubarb in tarts and ate it!

Well, I have discovered since that this is actually so. People really do grow it in their gardens, not with the idea of keeping the sun off the young carnations but under the impression that it is a fruit. Consequently, I have found it necessary to adopt a firm line with my friends' rhubarb. On arriving at any house for a visit, the first thing I say to my host is, 'May I see your rhubarb bed? I have heard such a lot about it.'

'By all means,' he says, feeling rather flattered, and leads the way into the garden.

'What a glorious sunset,' I say, pointing to the west.

'Isn't it,' he says, turning round; and then I surreptitiously drop a pint of weed-killer on the bed.

Next morning I get up early and paint the roots of the survivors with iodine.

Once my host, who for some reason had got up early too, discovered me.

'What are you doing?' he asked.

'Just painting the roots with iodine,' I said, 'to prevent the rhubarb falling out.'

'To prevent what?'

'To keep the green fly away,' I corrected myself. 'It's the new French intensive system.'

But he was suspicious, and I had to leave two or three stalks untreated. We had those for lunch that day. There was only one thing for a self-respecting man to do. I obtained a large plateful of the weed and emptied the sugar basin and the cream jug over it. Then I took a mouthful of the pastry, gave a little start, and said, 'Oh, is this rhubarb? I'm sorry, I didn't know.' Whereupon I pushed my plate away and started on the cheese.

A A MILNE *Those Were the Days*
1929

RHUBARB TED

I knew a funny little man
His name was Rhubarb Ted;
They called him that because he wore
Rhubarb on his head.

I'd grown so used to this strange sight,
The cause I did not seek;
But then one day to my surprise,
I saw he wore a leek.

I asked him if he'd please explain,
And let me know the reason;
He said, 'I'm wearing leek because
Rhubarb's out of season!'

ANN O'CONNOR

ROMANCE

I'm not quite sure about gardens being a good setting for romance. All right if you're just visiting, wandering around on a warm, starry night, enjoying the moonlight and the exotic scents. Not so good when husband and wife are struggling with the weeding and pruning and getting irritable with each other as their backs begin to go and the secateurs blister their hands.

I have included here an extract from Tennyson's poem *Maud*. The line 'Come into the garden Maud' must be one of the best known in the English language. It says everything about the garden as a setting for romance and Joyce Grenfell's parody reply says quite a lot about the age-old battle of the sexes.

COME INTO THE GARDEN MAUD

I

Come into the garden, Maud,
   For the black bat, night, has flown,
Come into the garden, Maud,
   I am here at the gate alone;
And the woodbine spices are wafted abroad,
   And the musk of the rose is blown.

II

For a breeze of morning moves,
  And the planet of Love is on high,
Beginning to faint in the light that she loves,
  On a bed of daffodil sky,
To faint in the light of the sun she loves,
  To faint in his light, and to die.

III

All night have the roses heard
  The flute, violin, bassoon;
All night has the casement jessamine stirr'd
  To the dancers dancing in tune;
Till a silence fell with a waking bird,
  And a hush with the setting moon.

IV

I said to the lily, 'There is but one
  With whom she has heart to be gay.
When will the dancers leave her alone?
  She is weary of dance and play.'
Now half to the setting moon are gone,
  And half to the rising day;
Low on the sand and loud on the stone
  The last wheel echoes away.

V

I said to the rose, 'The brief night goes
  In babble and revel and wine.
O young lord-lover, what sighs are those,
  For one that will never be thine?
But mine, but mine,' so I sware to the rose,
  'For ever and ever, mine.'

ALFRED LORD TENNYSON
1855

187

MAUD REPLIES . . .

Maud won't come into the garden
Maud is compelled to state.
Though you stand for hours in among the flowers
Down by the garden gate.
Maud won't come into the garden,
Sing to her as you may.
Maud says she begs your pardon
But she wasn't born yesterday.

But Maud's not coming into the garden
Thanking you just the same.
Though she looks so pure, you may be quite sure
Maud's on to your little game.
Maud knows she's being dampening,
And how damp you already must be,
So Maudie is now decamping
To her lovely hot water b.

Frankly, Maud wouldn't dream of coming into the garden,
Let that be understood,
When the nights are warm, Maud knows the form,
Maud has read 'Little Red Riding Hood'.
Maud did not need much warning,
She watched you with those pink gins,
So she bids you a kind 'Good Morning'
And advises you two aspirins.

You couldn't really seriously think that Maud was going to be such
                        a sucker as to come into the garden,

Flowers set her teeth on edge
And she's much too old for the strangle hold
In a prickly privet hedge.
Pray stand till your arteries harden
It won't do the slightest good,
Maud is not coming into the garden
And you're mad to have thought she would!

JOYCE GRENFELL

188

MR ROCHESTER'S GARDEN

I walked a while on the pavement; but a subtle, well-known scent—that of a cigar—stole from some window; I saw the library casement open a handbreadth; I knew I might be watched thence; so I went apart into the orchard. No nook in the grounds more sheltered and more Eden-like; it was full of trees, it bloomed with flowers: a very high wall shut it out from the court, on one side; on the other, a beech avenue screened it from the lawn. At the bottom was a sunk fence; its sole separation from lonely fields: a winding walk, bordered with laurels and terminating in a giant horse-chestnut, circled at the base by a seat, led down to the fence. Here one could wander unseen. While such honey-dew fell, such silence reigned, such gloaming gathered, I felt as if I could haunt such shade for ever: but in threading the flower and fruit-parterres at the upper part of the inclosure, enticed there by the light the now-risen moon casts on this more open quarter, my step is stayed—not by sound, not by sight, by once more by a warning fragrance.

Sweet briar and southernwood, jasmine, pink, and rose, have long been yielding their evening sacrifice of incense: this new scent is neither of shrub nor flower; it is—I know it well—it is Mr Rochester's cigar. I look around and I listen. I see trees laden with ripening fruit. I hear a nightingale warbling in a wood half a mile off; no moving form is visible, no coming step audible; but that perfume increases: I must flee. I make for the wicket leading to the shrubbery, and I see Mr Rochester entering. I step aside into the ivy recess, he will not stay long: he will soon return whence he came, and if I sit still he will never see me.

But no—eventide is as pleasant to him as to me, and this antique garden as attractive; and he strolls on, now lifting the gooseberry-tree branches to look at the fruit, large as plums, with which they are laden; now taking a ripe cherry from the wall; now stooping towards a knot of flowers, either to inhale their fragrance or to admire the dew-beads on their petals. A great moth goes humming by me: it alights on a plant at Mr Rochester's foot: he sees it, and bends to examine it.

'Now, he has his back towards me,' thought I, 'and he is occupied too; perhaps, if I walk softly, I can slip away unnoticed.'

I trod on an edging of turf that the crackle of the pebbly gravel might not betray me: he was standing among the beds at a yard or two distant from where I had to pass; the moth apparently engaged him. 'I shall get by very well,' I meditated. As I crossed his shadow, thrown long over the garden by the moon, not yet risen high, he said quietly without turning:--

'Jane, come and look at this fellow.'

CHARLOTTE BRONTË *Jane Eyre*

My beloved spake, and said unto me, Rise up, my love, my fair one,
    and come away.
For lo, the winter is past, the rain is over, and gone.
The flowers appear on the earth, the time of the singing of birds is
    come, and the voice of the turtle is heard in our land.
The fig tree putteth forth her green figs, and the vines with the
    tender grape give a good smell.
Arise, my love, my fair one, and come away.

The Song of Solomon

ROSES

'A rose is not a cabbage,' said D H Lawrence. Blindingly obvious really, but the point is that roses are divine and cabbages are not. To my mind no garden is complete without roses, and if I could choose just one type of flower it would have to be the rose. I have a friend in New England, a really keen gardener, but the cold winters make roses an impossibility for him. He has all my sympathy.

That consummate gardener Cyril Fletcher is a great rose man and everything he has to say on the subject is well worth reading not just for the first rate information but for the wonderful way he has with words.

OF ROSES

The Rose is surely the Queen of Flowers. It is a flower apart. There is a wonder about it. Pick an opening bud of a 'Papa Meilland' rose; it is the darkest of reds, and in its innermost recesses it is a shadowy black. Breathe in its perfume: it is velvet to touch and velvet-scented on the air. Next to your skin it is velvet again – no, it is veined satin. It is best to make this appraisal in the evening, an incense laden summer evening, the air close and the sun redly setting in the west. This rose suddenly has your undivided attention. Has it a secret to unfold? A message to deliver. This is a distillation from the earth. This is beauty. 'A sudden gladness gleams on the soul', wrote Coleridge. You will have shared a magical spiritual experience with the essence of the garden. A rose is more than just a flower. It brings with it a glimmer of the whys and wherefores of Creation. There must be an inner meaning to the mystery of their loveliness.

CYRIL FLETCHER *Cyril Fletcher's Rose Book*

'Would you tell me,' said Alice, a little timidly, 'why you are painting the roses?'

Five and Seven said nothing but looked at Two. Two began in a low voice, 'Why, the fact is, you see, Miss, this here ought to have been a *red* rose-tree, and we put in a white one by mistake.'

LEWIS CARROLL *Through the Looking-glass*

ROZIZ

And this is certain; if so be
You could just now my garden see,
The aspic of my flowers so bright
Would make you shudder with delight.

And if you voz to see my roziz
As is a boon to all men's noziz, –
You'd fall upon your back and scream –
'O Lawk! O criky! it's a dream!'

EDWARD LEAR

What's in a name? That which we call a
   rose
By any other word would smell as sweet.

WILLIAM SHAKESPEARE *Romeo and Juliet*

THE SICK ROSE

O Rose thou art sick.
The invisible worm
That flies in the night
In the howling storm,

Has found out thy bed
Of crimson joy:
And his dark secret love
Does thy life destroy.

WILLIAM BLAKE

I couldn't resist this wonderfully sentimental parlour song which was one of the great hits of 1813. Picture the scene. After dinner an enraptured group sits in the drawing room while our fine young tenor, with luxuriantly curling moustachios, is singing. Accompanying him at the pianoforte is a flower-like young girl who nurtures a secret, hopeless passion for him. For her the song contains a hidden meaning. . . .

THE LAST ROSE OF SUMMER

'Tis the last rose of summer
    Left blooming alone,
All her lovely companions
    Are faded and gone!
No flower of her kindred,
    No rosebud is nigh
To reflect back her blushes,
    Or give sigh for sigh.

I'll not leave thee, thou lone one,
    To pine on the stem;
Since the lovely are sleeping,
    Go, sleep thou with them:
Thus kindly I scatter
    Thy leaves o'er the bed
Where thy mates of the garden
    Lie scentless and dead.

So soon may I follow,
　When friendships decay,
And from love's shining circle,
　The gems drop away,
When true hearts lie wither'd,
　And fond ones are flown,
Oh! who would inhabit
　This bleak world alone.

THOMAS MOORE
1813

Man was made for better things than pruning his rose trees.

COLIN WILSON

ST JAMES'S PARK

Another one of those brilliant letters to *The Times*. I must say I think the idea of farmers keeping animals in the middle of the city would be an excellent way of keeping town dwellers in touch with the realities of nature. That Merry Monarch, Charles II, used to keep cows in St James's Park three hundred years ago. Like Mr E W Brabrook he used to stop off for light refreshment direct from the cow herself. In the king's case things were spiced up a bit by placing a little wine and sugar into the basin into which the cow was milked, so that an instant, frothy syllabub was produced. So much for your new-fangled frothy coffee machines!

COWS IN ST JAMES'S PARK

Sir,

It was with something like distress that, in coming here this morning through St James's Park, I missed the one piece of evidence of picturesque custom of which that park could boast.

Sixty or so years ago it was one of the 'delights of my youth.' passing through the park, to stop for a cup of milk and see it drawn from the cow; and I am sorry that it should now be 'the fallacious aspiration of my riper years.'

To us city boys it was almost our only chance of seeing a cow in the flesh. It is now, or was till yesterday, the only remaining evidence of the 'Spring Gardens' that once were so famous.

I hope that the authorities will restore the cows to their wonted place. To remove them is a tyrannous action to others than their proprietors, and it does not mend the matter that it has been necessary to call in the prerogative of his Majesty to justify the doing of an act that a private proprietor could not have lawfully done.

I have the honour to be, Sir, your most obedient humble servant.

Mr E W Brabrook to *The Times*
11 February 1905

SECRET GARDENS

I remember reading *The Secret Garden* in class at school and I vividly recall how exciting it was to be a child who rediscovers a secret, unknown garden locked away and forgotten behind a tall wall. When I was in Alan Bennett's adaptation of *Wind in the Willows* I re-read Kenneth Grahame's classic book. The enchanting thing about the book is the wonderful world it creates of the animals living in their own houses, unbeknown to we human beings. Badger's house is deep in the woods, Ratty, a boating sort of a fellow, lives on the river bank, but Mole has a totally hidden house and courtyard and he suffers terribly from homesickness when he is away. I love this moment when he finally persuades Ratty to come back with him to see his own little home.

MOLE'S GARDEN

The Mole struck a match, and by its light the Rat saw that they were standing in an open space, neatly swept and sanded underfoot, and directly facing them was Mole's little front door, with 'Mole End' painted, in gothic lettering, over the bell-pull at the side.

Mole reached down a lantern from a nail on the wall and lit it, and the Rat, looking round him, saw that they were in a sort of fore-court. A garden-seat stood on one side of the door, and on the other, a roller; for the Mole, who was a tidy animal when at home, could not stand having his ground kicked up by other animals into little runs that ended in earth-heaps. On the walls hung wire baskets with ferns in them, alternating with brackets carrying plaster statuary – Garibaldi, and the infant Samuel, and Queen Victoria, and other heroes of modern Italy. Down one side of the fore-court ran a skittle-alley, with benches along it and little wooden tables marked with rings that hinted at beer-mugs. In the middle was a small round pond containing goldfish and surrounded by a cockle-shell border. Out of the centre of the pond rose a fanciful erection clothed in more cockle-shells and topped by a large silvered glass ball that reflected everything all wrong and had a very pleasing effect.

KENNETH GRAHAME *The Wind in the Willows*
1908

THE SECRET GARDEN

Mary had stepped close to the robin, and suddenly the gust of wind swung aside some loose ivy trails, and more suddenly still she jumped towards them and caught them in her hand. This she did because she had seen something under them – a round knob which had been covered by the leaves hanging over it. It was the knob of a door.

She put her hands under the leaves and began to pull and push them aside. Thick as the ivy hung, it nearly all was a loose and swinging curtain, though some had crept over wood and iron. Mary's heart began to thump and her hands to shake a little in her delight and excitement. The robin kept singing and twittering away and tilting his head on one side, as if he were as excited as she was. What was this under her hands which was square and made of iron and which her fingers found a hole in?

It was the lock of the door which had been closed ten years, and she put her hand in her pocket, drew out the key, and found it fitted the keyhole. She put the key in and turned it. It took two hands to do it, but it did turn.

And then she took a long breath and looked behind her up the long walk to see if anyone was coming. No one was coming. No one ever did come, it seemed, and she took another long breath, because she could not help it, and she held back the swinging curtain of ivy and pushed back the door which opened slowly – slowly.

Then she slipped through it, and shut it behind her, and stood with her back against it, looking about her and breathing quite fast with excitement, and wonder, and delight.

She was standing *inside* the secret garden.

It was the sweetest, most mysterious-looking place anyone could imagine. The high walls which shut it in were covered with the leafless stems of climbing roses, which were so thick that they were matted together. Mary Lennox knew they were roses because she had seen a great many roses in India. All the ground was covered with grass of a wintry brown, and out of it grew clumps of bushes which were surely rose-bushes if they were alive. There were numbers of standard roses which had so spread their branches that they were like little trees. There were other trees in the garden, and one of the things that made the place look strangest and loveliest was that climbing roses had run all over them and swung down long tendrils which made light swaying curtains, and here and there they had caught at each other or at a far-reaching branch and had crept from one tree to another and made lovely bridges of themselves. There was neither leaves nor roses on them now, and Mary did not know whether they were dead or alive, but their thin grey or brown branches and sprays looked like a sort of hazy mantle spreading over everything, walls, and trees, and even brown grass, where they had fallen from their fastenings and run along the ground. It was this hazy tangle from tree to tree which made it look so mysterious. Mary had thought it must be different from other gardens which had not been left all by themselves so long; and, indeed, it was different from any other place she had ever seen in her life.

'How still it is!' she whispered. 'How still!'

Then she waited a moment and listened at the stillness. The robin, who had flown to his tree-top, was still as all the rest. He did not even flutter his wings; he sat without stirring and looked at Mary.

'No wonder it is still,' she whispered again, 'I am the first person who has spoken in here for ten years.'

She moved away from the door, stepping as softly as if she were afraid of awakening someone. She was glad that there was grass under her feet and that her steps made no sound. She walked under one of the fairy-like arches between the trees and looked up at the tendrils and sprays which formed them.

'I wonder if they are all quite dead,' she said. 'Is it all a quite dead garden? I wish it wasn't.'

But she was *inside* the wonderful garden, and she could come through the door under the ivy at any time, and she felt she had found a world all her own.

The sun was shining inside the four walls and the high arch of blue sky over this particular piece of Misselthwaite seemed even more brilliant and soft than it was over the moor. The robin flew down from his tree-top and hopped about or flew after her from one bush to another. He chirped a good deal and had a very busy air, as if he were showing her things. Everything was strange and silent, and she seemed to be hundreds of miles away from anyone, but somehow she did not feel lonely at all. All that troubled her was her wish that she knew whether all the roses were dead, or if perhaps some of them had lived and might put out leaves and buds as the weather got warmer. She did not want it to be a quite dead garden. If it were a quite alive garden, how wonderful it would be, and what thousands of roses would grow on every side!

Her skipping-rope had hung over her arm when she came in, and after she had walked about for a while she thought she would skip round the whole garden, stopping when she wanted to look at things. There seemed to have been grass paths here and there, and in one or two corners there were alcoves of evergreen with stone seats or tall moss-covered flower-urns in them.

As she came near the second of these alcoves she stopped skipping. There had once been a flower-bed in it, and she thought she saw something sticking out of the black earth – some sharp little pale green points. She remembered what Ben Weatherstaff had said, and she knelt down to look.

'Yes, they are tiny growing things and they *might* be crocuses or snowdrops or daffodils,' she whispered.

FRANCES HODGSON BURNETT *The Secret Garden*
1907

THE SUNKEN GARDEN

Speak not—whisper not;
Here bloweth thyme and bergamot;
Softly on the evening hour,
Secret herbs their spices shower,
Dark-spiked rosemary and myrrh,
Lean-stalked, purple lavender;
Hides within her bosom, too,
All her sorrows, bitter rue.

Breathe not—trespass not;
Of this green and darkling spot,
Latticed from the moon's beams,
Perchance a distant dreamer dreams;
Perchance upon its darkening air,
The unseen ghosts of children fare,
Faintly swinging, sway and sweep,
Like lovely sea-flowers in its deep;
While, unmoved, to watch and ward,
'Mid its gloom'd and daisied sward,
Stands with bowed and dewy head
That one little leaden Lad.

WALTER DE LA MARE

SLUGS AND SNAILS

SLUGS

Daisy Quantock was busy, like everybody else in the village on this beautiful afternoon of spring, with her garden, hacking about with a small but destructive fork in her flower-beds. She was a gardener of the ruthless type, and went for any small green thing that incautiously showed a timid spike above the earth, suspecting it of being a weed. She had had a slight difference with the professional gardener who had hitherto worked for her on three afternoons during the week, and had told him that his services were no longer required. She meant to do her gardening herself this year, and was confident that a profusion of beautiful flowers and a plethora of delicious vegetables would be the result. At the end of her garden path was a barrow of rich manure, which she proposed, when she had finished the slaughter of the innocents, to dig into the depopulated beds. On the other side of her paling her neighbour, Georgie Pillson, was rolling his strip of lawn, on which, during the summer, he often played croquet on a small scale. Occasionally they shouted remarks to each other, but as they got more and more out of breath with their exertions the remarks got fewer. Mrs Quantock's last question had been 'What do you do with slugs, Georgie?' and Georgie had panted out, 'Pretend you don't see them.'

E F BENSON *Lucia in London*
1927

THE SNAIL

At sunset, when the night-dews fall,
Out of the ivy on the wall
With horns outstretched and pointed tail
Comes the grey and noiseless snail.
On ivy stems she clambers down,
Carrying her house of brown.
Safe in the dark, no greedy eye
Can her tender body spy,
While she herself, a hungry thief,
Searches out the freshest leaf.
She travels on as best she can
Like a toppling caravan.

JAMES REEVES

THE SNAIL

... the snail, whose tender horns being hit,
Shrinks backward in his shelly cave with pain,
And there, all smother'd up, in shade doth sit,
Long after fearing to creep forth again:

WILLIAM SHAKESPEARE

THE SNAYLE

Is a Gentleman every inch of him; as ancient surely as Adams time; while for Armes, hee hath had a house for Coat ever since, which he bears to this day. He seemes very stately in the manner of his gate, but hee is not proud. He is cold of complexion, because flegmaticke, which makes him so slow of his pace. Hee is a Scholler, for he keepes his study, though he have no bookes. He is no Accademicke, though a Philosopher, because not sociable, but rather a Peripateticke, because a walker; but especially a Stoicke, because he carries all whatsoever hee hath on his backe. If hee were confined to his five miles according to the statute, it would trouble him nothing, while hee would travaile where hee list, yet not incurre the forfeiture, or the penalty of the law. He hath indeed a certaine house of his owne, but not a setled one, and a faire porch to it, but no doore. Hee is a free-holder, and no tenant at will, or for any terme that is lesse than his life. There is no covenant servants amongst them, but are householders every one. They have no constant Cities of their owne, while their houses joyne not one to another, as others doe. Though they wander much, and gad abroad, yet they are not included in the Statute of rogues. The Snayle and the Periwincle are much alike, with this difference, that the Snayle with paines carries his house on his backe, and the Periwincle, house and all, is carried with the waves with ease, as held up by the chinne. In fine, they are at peace with all the world, and have no enimies at all; and so like the Hamburgers, trade and travaile where they please; unless in a time of famine, when perhaps for better food, they come to be snapt up and made good prize.

ANON
1634

SNOWDROPS

My wife has grown a fine patch of Solomon's Seal in our garden. Recently she bought me Geoffrey Grigson's great book *The Englishman's Flora*, which contains, among many delights, ancient local nicknames for wild flowers. These have given us a good deal of pleasure and hilarity. We found that the somewhat solemnly named Solomon's Seal was at one time known less delicately as Sow's Tits! Here are other favourites from the book. Monkshood was called Lady Lavinia's Dove Carriage. Red Campion was called either Jack in the Hedge or Robin in the Hedge or Robin Hood and in Yorkshire, amazingly, Lousy Soldier's Buttons. Heartsease, or Wild Poppy, was called Kiss and Look Up in Somerset, Kiss at the Garden Gate in Suffolk, Kiss *Behind* the Garden Gate in Warwickshire, Kiss Me *Over* the Garden Gate in Norfolk and Meet Her in the Entry, Kiss Her in the Buttery in Lincolnshire – though I find it hard to believe that many people had the time or energy to give it its full name after first acquaintance.

Most obscure of all was the unlikely name given to Wall Pepper or Golden Moss – Welcome Home Husband Though Never So Drunk! I wouldn't be without that book.

Here dear, gentle Canon Ellacombe, author of the gardening classic *In a Gloucestershire Garden* ponders the many names given to the snowdrop.

Something must be said about the pretty name, or rather the pretty names, of the snowdrop. The common name is not the old name, and certainly, to nearly the end of the seventeenth century, it was described as the white bulbous violet. Such a cumbrous name might do when the plant was only a garden plant, and probably not a common one, but when it increased and multiplied so as to be found in every garden, and was becoming naturalized in many places, another name was wanted, and none more fitting could be found that the pretty name of snowdrop, which was creeping in Gerard's time (he gives the name very doubtfully), but which only came into general use by very slow degrees. I suppose it was adopted from the common names of the flower in its native countries, such as France and Germany. Its German names may be translated as snowflake, February flower, naked maiden-snow-violet, and snow-drop; and its French names as the white bell, the bell of the snows, the bell of winter, and the snow-piercer.

CANON ELLACOMBE *In a Gloucestershire Garden*
1895

And here's an amusing little pun on flower names:

I USED TO LOVE MY GARDEN

I used to love my garden
But now my love is dead
For I found a batchelor's button
In black-eyed Susan's bed.

C P SAWYER

SPRING

Hey Nonny Nonny it's springtime. Somehow the mere mention of spring and all the poets seem to get themselves into a frenzy.

SPRING

Spring, the sweet Spring, is the year's pleasant king;
Then blooms each thing, then maids dance in a ring,
Cold doth not sting, the pretty birds do sing:
Cuckoo, jug-jug, pu-we, to-witta-woo!

The palm and may make country houses gay,
Lambs frisk and play, the shepherds pipe all day;
And we hear aye birds tune this merry lay:
Cuckoo, jug-jug, pu-we, to-witta-woo!

The fields breathe sweet, the daisies kiss our feet,
Young lovers meet, old wives a-sunning sit,
In every street these tunes our ear do greet:
Cuckoo, jug-jug, pu-we, to-witta-woo!
    Spring, the sweet Spring!

THOMAS NASHE

One of the most pleasing sounds of Springtime to be heard all over the country, is the contented cooing of osteopaths as Man picks up his garden spade.

OLIVER PRITCHETT

What a man needs in gardening is a cast-iron back with a hinge on it.

CHARLES DUDLEY WARNER

LOVELIEST OF TREES, THE CHERRY NOW

Loveliest of trees, the cherry now
Is hung with bloom along the bough,
And stands about the woodland ride
Wearing white for Eastertide.

Now, of my threescore years and ten,
Twenty will not come again,
And take from seventy springs a score,
It only leaves me fifty more.

And since to look at things in bloom
Fifty springs are little room,
About the woodlands I will go
To see the cherry hung with snow.

A E HOUSMAN *A Shropshire Lad*

SPRING

Nothing is so beautiful as Spring —
  When weeds, in wheels, shoot long and lovely and lush;
  Thrush's eggs look little low heavens, and thrush
Through the echoing timber does so rinse and wring
The ear, it strikes like lightnings to hear him sing;
  The glassy peartree leaves and blooms, they brush
  The descending blue; that blue is all in a rush
With richness; the racing lambs too have fair their fling.

GERARD MANLEY HOPKINS

SPRING DAY

The Cock is crowing,
The stream is flowing,
　The small birds twitter,
　The lake doth glitter,
The green field sleeps in the sun;
　The oldest and youngest
　Are at work with the strongest;
　The cattle are grazing,
　Their heads never raising;
There are forty feeling like one!

　Like an army defeated
　The snow hath retreated,
　And now doth fare ill
　On the top of the bare hill;
The ploughboy is whooping—anon—anon:
　There's joy in the mountains;
　There's life in the fountains;
　Small clouds are sailing,
　Blue sky prevailing;
The rain is over and gone!

WILLIAM WORDSWORTH

I would I had some flowers o'th' spring that might
Become your time of day; and yours and yours,
That wear upon your virgin branches yet
Your maidenheads growing: O Proserpina,
For the flowers now, that frighted thou let'st fall
From Dis's waggon! daffodils,
That come before the swallow dares, and take
The winds of March with beauty; violets (dim,
But sweeter than the lids of Juno's eyes
Or Cytherea's breath); pale primroses,
That die unmarried, ere they can behold
Bright Phoebus in his strength (a malady
Most incident to maids); bold oxlips and
The crown imperial; lilies of all kinds,
The flower-de-luce being one! O, these I lack,
To make you garlands of –

WILLIAM SHAKESPEARE *The Winter's Tale*

One sunny time in May
When lambs were sporting
The sap ran in the spray
And I went courting,
And all the apple boughs
Were bright with blossoms
I picked an early rose
For my love's bosom.

JOHN MASEFIELD *The Country Scene*

SUMMER

Summer is a funny old season in this country. Some years all you can do is sit indoors watching the rain and wind lash your prize plants and knock them to the ground. (Wimbledon fortnight is a betting man's favourite for hurricane style weather over the southern counties.) Twelve months later, having battened down the hatches and shrubbery in preparation for arctic conditions, you find yourself with topsoil like face powder, plants drooping and parched and, inevitably, a hose-pipe ban. As a mere amateur gardener and meteorologist, my view is that on the whole summer temperatures have been rising. I am now less inclined to plant hydrangeas, which I used to regard as an ideal London shrub. It breaks my heart to watch them wilting after a day or two without water. I haven't yet got around to planting a garden of bougainvillaea and lavender but who knows what the future has in store?

SUMMER HEAT

Not a human being was out of doors at the dairy. . . . At the door the wood-hooped pails, sodden and bleached by infinite scrubbings, hung like hats on a stand upon the forked and peeled limb of an oak fixed there for that purpose; all of them ready and dry for the evening milking. . . . Sustained snores came from the cart-house, where some of the men were lying down; the grunt and squeal of sweltering pigs arose from the still further distance. The large rhubarb and cabbage plants slept too, their broad limp surfaces hanging in the sun like half-closed umbrellas.

THOMAS HARDY *Tess of the D'Urbervilles*

CUT GRASS

Cut grass lies frail:
Brief is the breath
Mown stalks exhale.
Long, long the death

It dies in the white hours
Of young-leafed June
With chestnut flowers,
With hedges snowlike strewn,

White lilac bowed,
Lost lanes of Queen Anne's lace,
And that high-builded cloud
Moving at summer's pace.

PHILIP LARKIN

AH! SUNFLOWER

Ah, Sunflower! weary of time,
Who countest the steps of the Sun,
Seeking after that sweet golden clime
Where the traveller's journey is done:

Where the Youth pined away with desire,
And the pale Virgin shrouded in snow
Arise from their graves, and aspire
Where my Sunflower wishes to go.

WILLIAM BLAKE

TOPIARY

You would think topiary was the ideal hobby for a committed hedge clipper like myself. The truth is I've never had the nerve to launch out into strange shapes but I think they are wonderful when other people do them. I like the classic feel which pyramids and pom-poms shapes give a garden. Visiting great gardens I love to see the mad shapes – cups and saucers, Mickey Mouse, hedgehogs and peacocks, which someone has patiently groomed into shape over the years. There are two strongly opposed schools of thought on the subject of topiary. You love it or you hate it. Eighteenth-century poet and gardening fanatic Alexander Pope hated it. His list of laughable subjects to be found in topiary form is still good for a laugh today.

A LAUGHABLE CATALOGUE OF GREENS TO BE DISPOSED OF BY AN EMINENT TOWN GARDENER

Adam and Eve in Yew; Adam a little shatter'd by the fall of the tree of Knowledge in the Great Storm. Eve and the Serpent very flourishing. The Tower of Babel not yet finished. St George in Box: his Arm scarce long enough, but will be in a condition to stick the Dragon by next April. A Green Dragon of the same, with a Tail of Ground Ivy for the present. NB. These two not to be sold separately. Edward the Black Prince in Cypress. A Laurustine Bear in Blossom, with a Juniper Hunter in Berries. A pair of Giants, stunted, to be sold cheap. A Queen Elizabeth in Phylyraea [*Phyllyrea*] a little inclining to the green-sickness, but full of growth. Another Queen Elizabeth in Myrtle, which was very forward, but miscarried by being too near a Savine. An old Maid of Honour in Wormwood. A topping Ben Jonson in Laurel. Divers eminent Modern Poets in Bay, somewhat blighted, to be disposed of, a pennyworth. A quickset Hog, shot up into a Porcupine, by being forgot a week in rainy Weather. A Lavender Pigg with Sage growing in his Belly. Noah's ark in Holly; standing on the Mount; the ribs a little damaged for want of Water. A pair of Maidenheads in Firr, in great forwardness.

ALEXANDER POPE
1713

I doe not like Images Cut out in Juniper or other Garden stuffes: They be for Children. Little low Hedges, Round, like Welts, with some Pretty Pyramides, I like well.

SIR FRANCIS BACON

What right have we to deform things given us so perfect and lovely in form? No cramming of Chinese feet into impossible shoes is half so wicked as the wilful and brutal distortion of the beautiful forms of trees.

WILLIAM ROBINSON *The English Flower Garden*
1898

TREES

For me Alexander Pope summed it up beautifully when he wrote, 'A tree is a nobler object than a prince in his coronation robes.'

Men seldom plant trees till they begin to grow Wise, that is, till they grow Old and find by Experience the Prudence and Necessity of it.

JOHN EVELYN

THE TREES

The trees are coming into leaf
Like something almost being said;
The recent buds relax and spread,
Their greenness is a kind of grief.

Is it that they are born again
And we grow old? No, they die too.
Their yearly trick of looking new
Is written down in rings of grain.

Yet still the unresting castles thresh
In fullgrown thickness every May.
Last year is dead, they seem to say,
Begin afresh, afresh, afresh.

PHILIP LARKIN

I found this charming piece in the introduction to one of my old books on nature study:

TREES

Many, many years ago, when a rich Scotch landlord lay dying, he said to his only son, 'Jock, when you have nothing else to do, be sticking in a tree; it will aye be growing when you are sleeping.' He was a clever, far-seeing old man, Jock's father, for he knew that in course of time trees grow to be worth money, and that to plant a tree was a sure and easy way of adding a little more to the wealth he loved so dearly.

But a tree has another and a greater value to us and to the world than the price which a wood merchant will give for it as timber. Think what a dear familiar friend the tree has been in the life of man! How different many of our best-loved tales would be without the trees that played so large a part in the lives of our favourite heroes. Where could Robin Hood and his merry men have lived and hunted but under the greenwood tree? Without the forest of Arden what refuge would have sheltered the mischief-loving Rosalind and her banished father? How often do we think of the stately Oak and Linden trees into which good old Baucis and Philemon were changed by the kindly gods.

And do you remember what secrets the trees told us as we lay under their shady branches on the hot midsummer days, while the leaves danced and flickered against the blue, blue sky? Can you tell what was the charm that held us like a dream in the falling dusk as we watched their heavy masses grow dark and gloomy against the silvery twilight sky?

In a corner of a Cumberland farmyard there grew a noble tree whose roots struck deep into the soil, and whose heavy branches shadowed much of the ground. 'Why do you not cut it down?' asked a stranger; 'it seems so much in the way.' 'Cut it down!' the farmer answered passionately. 'I would sooner fall on my knees and worship it.' To him the tree had spoken of a secret unguessed by Jock's father and by many other people who look at the trees with eyes that cannot see. He had learned that the mystery of tree life is one with the mystery that underlies our own; that we share this mystery with the sea, and the sun, and the stars, and that by this mystery of life the whole world is 'bound with gold chains' of love 'about the feet of God.'

C E SMITH *Trees Shown to the Children* 1912

Trees are the best monuments that a man can erect to his own memory. They speak his praises without flattery, and they are blessings to children yet unborn.

LORD ORRERY TO THOMAS CAREW
15 May 1749

Of all the wonders of nature, a tree in summer is perhaps the most remarkable; with the possible exception of a moose singing 'Embraceable You' in spats.

WOODY ALLEN

BIRCHES

When I see birches bend to left and right
Across the lines of straighter darker trees,
I like to think some boy's been swinging them.
But swinging doesn't bend them down to stay
As ice-storms do. Often you must have seen them
Loaded with ice a sunny winter morning
After a rain. They click upon themselves
As the breeze rises, and turn many-colored
As the stir cracks and crazes their enamel.
Soon the sun's warmth makes them shed crystal shells
Shattering and avalanching on the snow-crust—
Such heaps of broken glass to sweep away
You'd think the inner dome of heaven had fallen.
They are dragged to the withered bracken by the load,
And they seem not to break; though once they are bowed
So low for long, they never right themselves:
You may see their trunks arching in the woods
Years afterwards, trailing their leaves on the ground
Like girls on hands and knees that throw their hair
Before them over their heads to dry in the sun.

ROBERT FROST

FRUIT TREES

Is it not a pleasant sight to behold a multitude of trees round about,
in decent form and order, bespangled and gorgeously apparelled
with green leaves, blooms and goodly fruits as with a rich robe of
embroidered work, or as hanging with some precious and costly
jewels or pearls, the boughs laden and burdened, bowing down to
you, and freely offering their ripe fruits as a large satisfaction of all
your labours?

RALPH AUSTEN *A Treatise of Fruit-Trees*,
1653

PINE TREES

A wind sways the pines,
    And below
Not a breath of wild air:
Still as the mosses that glow
On the flooring and under the lines
Of the roots here and there.
The pine-tree drops its dead;
They are quiet as under the sea.
Overhead, overhead
Rushes life in a race,
As the clouds the clouds chase;
    And we go,
And we drop like the fruits of the tree,
    Even we,
    Even so.

GEORGE MEREDITH

THE tree which moves some to tears of joy is in the eyes of others only a green thing which stands in the way ... As a man is, so he sees.

WILLIAM BLAKE

This American parlour song was inspired by an incident at the poet's old family home. When he went back to revisit his grandfather's house, where he had spent so many days, he found an old man about to chop down the tree he remembered so well. The man wanted to sell firewood for money. Morris paid him $10 and the woodman and his daughter promised to let the tree remain. The song was a big success on both sides of the Atlantic.

WOODMAN, SPARE THAT TREE

Woodman, spare that tree!
Touch not a single bough;
In youth it shelter'd me,
And I'll protect it now;
'Twas my forefather's hand
That placed it near his cot,
There, woodman, let it stand,
Thy axe shall harm it not!

That old familiar tree,
Whose glory and renown
Are spread o'er land and sea,
And wouldst thou hew it down?
Woodman, forbear thy stroke!
Cut not its earth-bound ties;
Oh! spare that aged oak
Now tow'ring to the skies!

When but an idle boy
I sought its grateful shade;
In all their gushing joy
Here, too, my sisters played.
My Mother kiss'd me here;
My Father press'd my hand —
Forgive this foolish tear,
But let that old oak stand!

My heart-strings round thee cling,
Close as thy bark, old friend!
Here shall the wild-bird sing
And still thy branches bend,
Old tree, the storm still brave!
And, woodman, leave the spot;
While I've a hand to save,
Thy axe shall harm it not.

GEORGE POPE MORRIS
1837

TULIPS

The disease tulipomania has been prevalent in Britain ever since the days of that famous monarch Williamnmary. William and his wife Mary were keen gardeners who introduced tulips to Britain from William's native Holland. I'm always a little wary of tulips myself. They are great beauties but for the easy life I prefer the idea of bulbs you can leave in the ground year after year to naturalize.

Something tells me that home-and-garden-loving Queen Mary back in the seventeenth century would have enjoyed the long-running radio programme *Mrs Dale's Diary* as much as her twentieth-century counterpart Queen Elizabeth the Queen Mother did. The Queen Mum found it a good way of keeping up with the interests and concerns of ordinary people! I loved the programme myself, especially when that great thirties star, Jessie Matthews, took over the main role. Now, of course, it strikes us as a real period piece and the younger generation doesn't know what you're talking about if you refer to it.

Along with the programme there was a whole series of books about Mrs Dale and her cosy lifestyle and this extract is taken from one of them. Monument, by the way, is Mrs D's gardener, a real treasure.

TULIPOMANIA

I suffer from Tulipomania. I would like, above all things, to see the tulips that grow wild along the northern shores of the Mediterranean, in Africa, in Asia and Japan, and I am always trying out—with Monument's permission—new sorts of tulips in the

garden. Tulips are so pleasant because you can plant them late, last of all the bulbs; just when you are regretting that you have not put in those other bulbs that you meant to have such a show with in the spring, and that you have left much too late, you remember the tulips! Although autumn has come, and winter is almost here, the wind is whistling and the trees are bare, it is not too late to put them in. But tulips are tricky things in one way, Monument has taught me that; they must always be lifted when they die off, as they leave a disease behind them, and the soil must be cleaned of it. Occasionally, though, we *do* leave them in, but Monument covers the ground with peat before they start to turn yellow, and he also does this if we are going to plant tulips in the same bed the following year. We have got an established stock of them now, and they multiply obligingly, but I still experiment with them, and have tulips in all sorts of out-of-the-way places in the garden and not just in a formal bed. There are dozens and dozens of kinds; besides the ordinary Darwins and cottage tulips, there are striped ones, frilled ones, lily-tulips, rockery tulips, tulips that can be naturalised in grass, tulips for pots and bowls, and little edging ones for massing along the front of a small bed or of the rockery.

Tulips are supposed to have come to England from Constantinople. First of all, only *one* tulip came; a sailor brought it home and gave it to the wife of an apothecary. He was a very poor sailor, and he had nothing at all to give her after she had nursed him when he was ill, then he remembered a dried-up-looking bulb that he had acquired casually on his travels. Why he only had one bulb I have no idea, but one was all he gave to the apothecary's wife. She put it in a pot and cultivated it most tenderly, then, as time went on, the tulip bulb increased itself. People came to see her pots of flowers, and she sold the bulbs for a guinea each. This was in the middle of the sixteenth century, and about the same time other sailors brought

tulips to Holland; there they became the fashion and the centre of a wild craze, which was known as 'tulipomania'. Nobody could grow enough tulips, nobody could talk of anything *but* tulips; the Dutch horticulturists sold the bulbs for fantastic prices, and made strange experiments, which resulted in the lovely striped and bizarre tulips that appear in flower pictures by the Dutch masters. These tulips are most exciting, and are called Bizarre, Biblomen, and Rembrandt. I am always adding a few to the ones we have. But I think that the occasion when I most thank the apothecary's wife for caring for her bulb so cleverly is when, in March and April, I look at the round bed in the front of our house. Each year there we put in the tulip species *T. fosteriana*—which is a wonderful flower, brilliant crimson with a dark centre. Who was she, I wonder, the unknown apothecary's wife? And was her single tulip pink, or red, or yellow—or even striped?

Jonquil Antony *Mrs Dale at Home*
1952

UNEXPECTED!

GARDEN SURPRISE

I shall never forget a visit to that nursery some six-and-twenty years ago. It was walled all round, and a deep-sounding bell had to be rung many times before anyone came to open the gate; but at last it was opened by a fine, strongly-built, sunburnt woman of the type of the good working farmer's wife, that I remember as a child. She was the forewoman, who worked the nursery with surprisingly few hands – only three men, if I remember rightly – but she looked as if she could do the work of 'all two men' herself. One of the specialities of the place was a fine breed of mastiffs; another was an old *Black Hamburg vine*, that rambled and clambered in and out of some very old greenhouses, and was wonderfully productive. There were alleys of nuts in all directions, and large spreading patches of palest yellow daffodils – the double *Narcissus cernuus* [double-flowered *N.c. plenus* white], now so scarce and difficult to grow. Had I then known how precious a thing was there in fair abundance, I should not have been contented with the modest dozen that I asked for. It was a most pleasant garden to wander in, especially with the old Mr Webb who presently appeared. He was dressed in black clothes of an old-looking cut – a Quaker, I believe. Never shall I forget an apple-tart he invited me to try as a proof of the merit of the 'Wellington' apple [now superseded by 'Bramley seedling']. It was not only good, but beautiful; the cooked apple looking rosy and transparent, and most inviting. He told me he was an ardent preacher of total abstinence, and took me to a grassy, shady place among the nuts, where there was an upright stone slab, like a tomb-stone, with the inscription:

TO ALCOHOL

He had dug a grave, and poured into it a quantity of wine and beer and spirits, and placed the stone as a memorial of his abhorrence of drink. The whole thing remains in my mind like a picture – the shady groves of old nuts, in tenderest early leaf, the pale daffodils, the mighty chained mastiffs with bloodshot eyes and murderous fangs, the brawny, wholesome forewoman, and the trim old gentleman in black. It was the only nursery I ever saw where one would expect to see fairies on a summer's night.

GERTRUDE JEKYLL *Wood and Garden*
1899

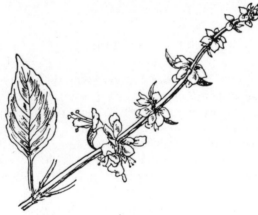

BASIL (GARDEN OR SWEET)

Hilarius, a French physician, affirms upon his own knowledge, that an acquaintance of his, by common smelling to it, had a scorpion bred in his brain.

NICHOLAS CULPEPER *Culpeper's Complete Herbal*
1653

MRS EARLE'S RECIPE FOR 'SWEET-BAGS' FOR ARMCHAIRS

On the backs of my armchairs are thin Liberty silk oblong bags, like miniature saddle-bags, filled with dried Lavender, Sweet Verbena, and Sweet Geranium leaves. The visitor who leans back in his chair wonders from where the sweet scent comes.

Pot-pourri from a Surrey Garden
1897

Nothing grows in our garden, only washing. And babies.

DYLAN THOMAS *Under Milk Wood*

AN UNANNOUNCED ARRIVAL

I was on the point of slinking off, to think how I had best proceed, when there came out of the house a lady with her handkerchief tied over her cap, and a pair of gardening gloves on her hands, wearing a gardening pocket like a toll-man's apron, and carrying a great knife. I knew her immediately to be Miss Betsey, for she came stalking out of the house exactly as my poor mother had so often described her stalking up our garden at Blunderstone Rookery.

'Go away!' said Miss Betsey, shaking her head, and making a

distant chop in the air with her knife. 'Go along! No boys here!'

I watched her, with my heart at my lips, as she marched to a corner of her garden, and stooped to dig up some little root there. Then, without a scrap of courage, but with a great deal of desperation, I went softly in and stood beside her, touching her with my finger.

'If you please, ma'am,' I began.

She started and looked up.

'If you please, aunt.'

'EH?' exclaimed Miss Betsey, in a tone of amazement I have never heard approached.

'If you please, aunt, I am your nephew.'

'Oh, Lord!' said my aunt. And sat flat down in the garden-path.

CHARLES DICKENS *David Copperfield*
1850

VAUXHALL
GARDENS

Playing Lord Foppington in Vanbrugh's amusing play *The Relapse* gave me a taste for seventeenth and eighteenth century comedy. I love the idea of all the fops, dandies and ladies of fashion strutting their stuff in the fashionable pleasure gardens at Vauxhall and Ranelagh. Sadlers Wells, where there is now an excellent theatre, was also one of London's many pleasure gardens. I'm sure the weather must have been milder then or they never would have made commercial sense, although having worn period costume I can vouch for the fact that it weighs a ton and would keep you warm on the coldest evening.

Trust that rascally ladies' man Pepys to witness a saucy incident on his visit to what was then known as Foxhall gardens. I imagine there must have been a lot of flirting (at the very least) going on in these places. Costume may change but life goes on pretty much the same as it always has done.

AN INCIDENT AT VAUXHALL PLEASURE GARDENS

By water to Fox-hall and there walked in Spring garden; a great deal of company and the weather and garden pleasant; that it is very pleasant and cheap going thither, for a man may go to spend what he will, or nothing, all as one – but to hear the nightingale and other birds, and here fiddles, and there a harp, and here a jews trump, and here laughing, and there fine people walking, is mighty divertising. Among others, there were two pretty women alone, that walked a great while: which, discovered by some idle gentlemen, they would needs take them up; but to see the poor ladies, how they were put to it to run from them, and they after them: and sometimes the ladies put themselves along with other company, then the others drew back; at last, the ladies did get off out of the house and took boat and away.

SAMUEL PEPYS *Diary*
28 May 1667

Even Bishops have been seen in this Recess without injuring their character.

A Guide to Vauxhall
1753

Ranelagh looks like the enchanted palace of a genie, adorned with the most exquisite performances of painting, carving and gilding . . . crowded with the great, the rich, the gay, the happy, the fair; glittering with cloth of gold and silver, lace, embroidery, amid precious stones . . .

TOBIAS SMOLLET *Humphry Clinker*
1770

VEGETABLES

One of the most enjoyable periods of my acting career was the television series *The Good Life*. In it I and my screen wife, played by the delightful Felicity Kendal, were shown struggling with the vicissitudes of nature and the prejudice of our middle-class neighbours, as we attempted to create a self-sufficient way of life in our suburban house and garden in the home counties. Although I never quite screwed up the courage to suggest to my *real* wife, Annie, that we establish a chicken coop and a goat on the lawn, I did find that during the second series I was overcome with a nagging urge to grow my own vegetables in my own back garden.

I dug up part of an old flower bed and started growing what I confidently anticipated (seduced by those seed catalogues again) would be large and luscious radishes, lettuces and runner beans. I'd just completed

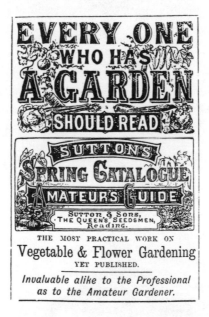

the sowing when my back began to seize up in agony, and it cost me over £50 in visits to the osteopath to get it put right.

Sometime later, restored to health, I was called away to do a month's filming. On my return I was shocked to find the runner beans running wild over the nearby trees. I spent a dangerous afternoon balanced on a dodgy ladder, with Annie squeaking at me from below, while I got them down again.

Subsequent inspection revealed that the birds and slugs between them had seen to the lettuces and radishes. I decided there and then that real life is *not* like television and reflected that I could have bought an awful lot of veggies for £50. So I turfed the bed over, planted a deckchair there instead, and went back to reading seed catalogues!

Botany, n. The science of vegetables – those that are not good to eat, as well as those that are. It deals largely with their flowers, which are commonly badly designed, inartistic in colour, and ill-smelling.

Cabbage, n. A familiar kitchen-garden vegetable about as large and wise as a man's head.

AMBROSE BIERCE *The Devil's Dictionary*
1911

THE CABBAGE

It is remarkable, that although there is no country in the world now more plentifully supplied with fruits and vegetables than Great Britain, yet the greater number of these had no existence in it before the time of Henry VIII. Anderson, writing under the date of 1548, says, 'The English cultivated scarcely any vegetables before the last two centuries. At the commencement of the reign of Henry VIII, neither salad, nor carrots, nor cabbages, nor radishes, nor any other comestibles of a like nature, were grown in any part of the kingdom; they came from Holland and Flanders.' The original of all the cabbage tribe is the wild plant *sea-colewort*, which is to be found *wasting* whatever sweetness it may have on the desert air, on many of the cliffs of the south coast of England. In this state, it scarcely weighs more than half an ounce, yet, in a cultivated state, to what dimensions can it be made to grow! However greatly the whole of the tribe is esteemed among the moderns, by the ancients they were held in yet higher estimation. The Egyptians adored and raised altars to them, and the Greeks and Romans ascribed many of the most exalted virtues to them. Cato affirmed, that the cabbage cured all diseases, and declared, that it was to its use that the Romans were enabled to live in health and without the assistance of physicians for

600 years. It was introduced by that people into Germany, Gaul, and, no doubt, Britain; although, in this last, it may have been suffered to pass into desuetude for some centuries. The whole tribe is in general wholesome and nutritive, and forms a valuable adjunct to animal food.

MRS BEETON
1861

A cauliflower is a cabbage with a college education.

MARK TWAIN

WATER

Is water in the garden a 'good thing' or a 'bad thing'? Does it add a wonderful new dimension, bringing tranquility, coolness and the opportunity to plant the wonderful range of plants that flourishes in a bog garden. Or does it mean weeds, frogs and midges?

Water was certainly a source of great pleasure to our late lamented cat, who regularly brought frogs into the kitchen. On one occasion she actually brought in a pair who were in the process of mating and were firmly attached to one another. Quite frequently she triumphantly dumped small, sodden green masses at our feet in the mistaken belief that she had caught a frog. In fact the frog had hopped off in the nick of time leaving her with the illusion of triumph and a mouthful of weed.

Having toyed with the idea of water for some time I recently allowed myself to be swayed by a close actor friend. He had created a pond in his garden and was extremely proud of it. Though a smallish, modest affair, it was very attractive and cost him next to nothing. I was fired by this example to have a pond myself, but thought I would have something grander in order to one-up him. I laid out a sizeable amount of cash and got the professionals in. The site was a dilapidated paved area in the centre of the garden.

The professionals dug down about three feet and to my utter joy discovered the remains of an original Victorian pond long-buried under the paving stones. At once my wife and I decided to restore it to its former glory. York stone arrived (more expense) and in a few weeks it was ready, complete with a small fountain in the middle which we felt added a touch of class.

In went the fish (fourteen chebunkins) who gave life to the still waters. I was delighted. Everything in the garden was lovely for a couple of

months until . . . the heron arrived. Fourteen chebunkins were rapidly reduced to seven who promptly and sensibly decided to submerge for the rest of their lives. My friend, whose pond was only a foot or so deep, could see his fish all the time. Since mine is three and a half feet deep, we only catch fleeting glimpses, except when they surface briefly to be fed.

Then a further threat arrived in the form of blanket weed which seems to enjoy this expensively re-constructed habitat even more than the fish. In fact, it has taken over the entire area.

Now, instead of spending my leisure hours placidly snoozing to the gentle sounds of the tinkling fountain, while the sun plays on the crystal surface of the pond, you will find me most days, leaning dangerously out over the dark green water, one bare arm submerged up to a freezing armpit, desperately tearing away at the weed. Behind me crouches my faithful wife, clinging to the back of my trousers to save me from the green and murky depths.

As for the stylish fountain, three crows have commandeered it as a bathing area. In the process of their energetic ablutions they have destroyed the nozzle which supplied the picturesque spray of water.

I had been close to despair and feeling rather humiliated that my childish attempt to outdo my friend had been so rapidly reversed when the same friend phoned in a state of some distress. Two stray dogs had made their way into his garden and had a fight, during which they had both fallen into his pond and destroyed it entirely. I suggested that the dogs may have mistaken *his* pond for a puddle. Had he had a professional pond of, say, three and a half feet deep such an accident could never have occurred. I have recovered my self-esteem but my friend hasn't been in touch with me for several months now.

For Fountains, they are a Great Beauty and Refreshment, but Pools mar all, and make the Garden unwholesome, and full of Flies and Frogs.

SIR FRANCIS BACON *Of Gardens*
1625

A fountain is most beautiful when it leaps high into the air, and you can see it against a background of green foliage.

HENRY ARTHUR BRIGHT *The English Flower Garden*
1881

OUR GOLDFISH

We have three goldfish in our pond
Of whom my father's very fond,
And they were given by his choice
The names of Julia, Edith, Joyce.

(Since many a year they did abide,
Nor added nor yet multiplied
It seemed a safe thing to report
They all were of one sex or sort.)

And Father feeds them every day,
And often has been heard to say
That Edith looked a little wan
Or Joyce more weight was putting on.

But Julia was his special friend;
She swam the pond from end to end,
So long, so strong, so golden-red —
The finest fish, so Father said.

The poet Herrick loved and sung
A Julia when he was young;
And Father knew a Julia too —
His cousin, hence his tribute true.

But now a sudden doubt arises,
One of life's tragical surprises:
A friend points out with sceptic air
That goldfish (girls) alas are rare.

A gloom across our pond is shed,
The water-lily droops its head,
The reeds are wilting on the brink
And nobody knows what to think.

Though Father still by word of voice
Addresses Julia, Edith, Joyce,
His tones the sad conviction carry
They might be Thomas, Dick and Harry.

Margaret Lodge

THE WONDER OF WATER

They climbed down a slippery bank of pine-needles. There lay the pond, set in its little alp of green – only a pond, but large enough to contain the human body, and pure enough to reflect the sky. On account of the rains, the waters had flooded the surrounding grass, which showed like a beautiful emerald path, tempting the feet towards the central pool.

'It's distinctly successful, as ponds go,' said Mr Beebe. 'No apologies are necessary for the pond.'

George sat down where the ground was dry, and drearily unlaced his boots.

'Aren't those masses of willow-herb splendid? I love willow-herb in seed. What's the name of this aromatic plant?'

No one knew or seemed to care.

'These abrupt changes of vegetation – this little spongeous tract of water-plants, and on either side of it all the growths are tough or brittle – heather, bracken, hurts, pines. Very charming, very charming.'

'Mr Beebe, aren't you bathing?' called Freddy, as he stripped himself.

Mr Beebe thought he was not.

'Water's wonderful!' cried Freddy, prancing in.

'Water's water,' murmured George. Wetting his hair first – a sure sign of apathy – he followed Freddy into the divine, as indifferent as if he were a statue and the pond a pail of soapsuds. It was necessary to use his muscles. It was necessary to keep clean. Mr Beebe watched them, and watched the seeds of the willow-herb dance chorically above their heads.

'Apooshoo, apooshoo, apooshoo,' went Freddy, swimming for two strokes in either direction, and then becoming involved in reeds or mud.

'Is it worth it?' asked the other, Michelangelesque on the flooded margin.

The bank broke away, and he fell into the pool before he had weighed the question properly.

'Hee – poof – I've swallowed a polly-wog. Mr Beebe, water's wonderful, water's simply ripping.'

'Water's not so bad,' said George, reappearing from his plunge, and sputtering at the sun.

'Water's wonderful. Mr Beebe, do.'

'Apooshoo, kouf.'

Mr Beebe, who was hot, and who always acquiesced where possible, looked around him. He could detect no parishioners except the pine trees, rising up steeply on all sides, and gesturing to each other against the blue. How glorious it was! The world of motor-cars and Rural Deans receded illimitably. Water, sky, evergreens, a wind – these things not even the seasons can touch, and surely they lie beyond the intrusion of man?

'I may as well wash too'; and soon his garments made a third little pile on the sward, and he too asserted the wonder of the water.

E M FORSTER *A Room With a View*
1908

238

WEATHER

The less said on this subject the better!

WEATHERS

I

This is the weather the cuckoo likes,
 And so do I;
When showers betumble the chestnut spikes,
 And nestlings fly:
And the little brown nightingale bills his best,
And they sit outside at 'The Travellers' Rest',
And maids come forth sprig-muslin drest,
And citizens dream of the south and west,
 And so do I.

II

This is the weather the shepherd shuns,
 And so do I;
When beeches drip in browns and duns,
 And thresh, and ply;
And hill-hid tides throb, throe on throe,
And meadow rivulets overflow,
And drops on gate-bars hang in a row,
And rooks in families homeward go,
 And so do I.

THOMAS HARDY

WEATHER WISDOM

I was brought up for the most part in the country, in a beautiful, wild, old-fashioned garden. This garden had remained in the hands of an old gardener for more than thirty years, which carries us back nearly a century. Almost all that has remained in my mind of my young days in this garden is how wonderfully the old man kept the place. He succeeded in flowering many things year after year with no one to help him, and with the frost in the valley to contend with in spring. It was difficult, too, for him to get seeds or plants, since the place was held by joint owners, whom he did not like to ask for them. The spot was very sheltered, and that is one of the greatest of all secrets for plant cultivation. An ever-flowing mill stream ran all round the garden; and the hedges of China-roses, Sweetbriar, Honeysuckle and white Hawthorn tucked their toes into the soft mud, and throve year after year. The old man was a philosopher in his way, and when on a cold March morning my sisters and I used to rush out after lessons and ask him what the weather was going to be, he would stop his digging, look up at the sky, and say: 'Well, Miss, it may be fine and it may be wet; and if the sun comes out, it will be warmer.' After this solemn announcement he would wipe his brow and resume his work, and we went off, quite satisfied, to our well-known haunts in the Hertfordshire woods . . .

THERESA EARLE *Pot-pourri From a Surrey Garden*
1897

WEEDS

Opinion is divided on the subject of weeds. Some would say that a weed is in the eye of the beholder and see beauty in the most ghastly plant which steals unnoticed into your flower bed or threatens the perfection of your well tended lawn. Others go to the opposite extreme and pounce on everything that shows an unscheduled head, thereby cutting down the chances of ever finding something really wonderful which has arrived by mistake – a phenomenon which to my mind is one of the great unsung pleasures of the gardening adventure.

On the subject of ground-elder however, I am immoveable. This is the weed to end all weeds. It represents an impossible challenge even to an unrepentant trimmer and clipper like myself.

The eradication of ground-elder is one of the great imponderables and impossibilities of our age, along with discovering an alcoholic drink that you can quaff all day without getting a hangover and fathoming the answer to the world's economic problems by next Tuesday.

Like many other simple, optimistic souls, I have dug it up, poisoned it, stamped on it, set fire to it and paid young relatives pounds of pocket money to spend hours unravelling it and pulling up its endless root network. All to no avail. Now I am resigned to clipping it down to ground level so that it doesn't show too much. It seems there is only one long term answer – move to another address which doesn't have any. There are some elder plants that seem quite virtuous: I am watching the garden of a friend who planted a rather pretty variegated elder with some trepidation. It could be the gardening equivalent of the Trojan horse.

Weed – a herb that Providence has planted in the wrong place.

FRED STREETER

A weed is a plant whose virtues have not yet been discovered.

RALPH WALDO EMERSON

As for hollyhocks at the cottage door, and honeysuckle and jasmine
You may go and whistle;
But the tailor's front garden grows two cabbages, a dock,
A ha'porthe of pennyroyal, two dandelions and a thistle.

TOM HOOD
1835–74

WINTER

Winter is a tricky time for gardeners. On the one hand those wretched weeds tend to die off, along with everything else – so that's a blessing. On the other hand, unless you are an absolute genius with your planting, planning wonderful berries and russet foliage, sheltered roses that somehow manage a bloom or two until a very hard frost and beautifully sited evergreen trees to give the view depth and structure, your garden can be rather a sorry sight.

I choose to look on the bright side. Conditions are against gardening so I can enjoy guilt-free time in the house, feeling snug and cosy, and browse through the seed catalogues. Needless to say my garden never quite achieves the glory depicted in the catalogues, with their illustrations of perfect blooms, unravaged by the little problems which nature can throw at you. But like gardeners everywhere I am spurred on by hope of perfection. Not surprisingly, both the following quotations gave me amusement and reassurance. If Vita Sackville-West could be caught out by those seductive brochures what chance does a mere amateur like myself have?

I have grown wise, after many years of gardening, and no longer order recklessly from wildly alluring descriptions which make every annual sound easy to grow and as brilliant as a film star. I now know that gardening is not like that.

VITA SACKVILLE-WEST *In Your Garden Again*
1953

WINTER

When icicles hang by the wall,
   And Dick the shepherd blows his nail,
And Tom bears logs into the hall,
   And milk comes frozen home in pail;
When blood is nipped, and ways be foul,
Then nightly sings the staring owl:
Tu-whit, tu-whoo! — a merry note,
While greasy Joan doth keel the pot.

When all aloud the wind doth blow,
   And coughing drowns the parson's saw,
And birds sit brooding in the snow,
   And Marian's nose looks red and raw;
When roasted crabs hiss in the bowl,
Then nightly sings the staring owl:
Tu-whit, tu-whoo! — a merry note,
While greasy Joan doth keel the pot.

WILLIAM SHAKESPEARE *Loves Labour's Lost*

ONE FIRM FAITH

I don't believe the half I hear
Nor the quarter of what I see!
But I have one faith, sublime and true,
That nothing can shake or slay;
Each spring I firmly believe anew
All the seed catalogues say!

CAROLINE WELLS

If December passes without snow, we indignantly demand to know
what has become of our good, old-fashioned winters, and talk as if
we had been cheated out of something we had bought and paid for;
and when it *does* snow, our language is a disgrace to a Christian
nation.

JEROME K JEROME

'Hurrah! blister my kidneys,' exclaimed he in delight. 'It is a frost! –
the dahlias are dead.'

R S SURTEES *Handley Cross*
1843

WOMEN

No doubt about it, women make marvellous gardeners. Jane Loudon, Gertrude Jekyll, Vita Sackville-West, Margery Fish, Penelope Hobhouse, and my friend Penelope Keith to name just a few. In fact they are all *so* marvellous that I have tried to suggest to Annie that I hand our garden over to her completely. I cannot understand why she doesn't want to take up this very generous offer.

An Englishman cannot help making a garden. And an English-woman cannot help tending it for him and with him.

CYRIL FLETCHER *Nice One Cyril*
1978

Few gardeners garden for the love of the garden. Most positively detest the sight of it. What then persuades a man to exchange the warmth and comfort of his hearth for the Passchendaele of the garden? Your immediate answer may be – the Little Woman.

WILLIAM RUSHTON *The Alternative Gardener*

The care of plants, such as needed peculiar care or skill to rear them, was the female province. Everyone in town or country had a garden. Into this garden no foot of man intruded after it was dug in the spring. I think I see yet what I so often beheld – a respectable mistress of a family going out to her garden, on an April morning, with her great calash, her little painted basket of seeds, and her rake over her shoulder, going to her gardens of labors. A woman in very easy circumstances and abundantly gentle in form and manners would sow and plant and rake incessantly.

MRS GRANT *Memoirs of an American Lady*
c 1760

In Marche and in Aprill,
from morning to night:
   in sowing and setting,
good huswives delight,
   To have in their garden or
some other plot:
   to trim up their house, and
to furnish their plot
   Have millions [melons] at
Michaelmas, parsneps in Lent:
   in June, buttred beans,
saveth fish to be spent
   With these and good
pottage inough having than:
   thou winnest the heart of
thy laboring man.

TOMAS TUSSER
Five Hundreth Pointes of Good Husbandrie
1573

YOUNG
GARDENERS

It seems appropriate to end a gardening anthology with something about young gardeners. A love of gardening often begins in childhood and with a little careful nurturing a whole new generation of enthusiastic gardeners will grow up to take over the good work. What a prophet Mr Shewell-Cooper turned out to be.

ROYAL LODGE WINDSOR

To keep these gardens quite private, there are planted up all round glorious flowering shrubs, and close to their little plots are two lovely aviaries where the Princesses [the future Elizabeth II and Princess Margaret] used to have their budgerigars. Each Princess used to have a little lawn, and in their gardens they grew heaths, montbretias, hydrangeas, aubretias, balm, baby azaleas and other flowers. They shared a very pretty sunken garden planted up with many different kinds of Alpines. They had their own sets of tools, a little tool-house and a little seat on which they used to sit to rest from their labours. They had their own little barrow as well as the hoes, rakes, brushes, and so on. The seat is of a type made by the Royal Wheelwrights, of Windsor oak and of a royal pattern. These seats are, as it were, a 'patent', and are used all over the Royal Park.

It was obvious that Prince Charles, though only two and a half years old at the time, insisted on having a baby garden of his own in the summer of 1951. He got some tiny little bricks about an inch square, and made a little path. He got a little bowl to form a miniature pool and put some more of his wee bricks at the back. I took a photograph of this also. Remember that in all it only measures eighteen inches or so — but, who knows, he may have inherited his grandfather's natural gift.

W E SHEWELL-COOPER *The Royal Gardeners*
1952

SCHOOL GARDEN

The garden was a wide enclosure, surrounded with walls so high as
to exclude every glimpse of prospect; a covered verandah ran down
one side, and broad walks bordered a middle space divided into
scores of little beds: these beds were assigned as gardens for the
pupils to cultivate, and each bed had an owner. When full of flowers
they would doubtless look pretty.

CHARLOTTE BRONTË *Jane Eyre*

LITTLE GARDENS

As spring came on, a new set of amusements became the fashion,
and the lengthening days gave long afternoons for work and play of
all sorts. The garden had to be put in order, and each sister had a

quarter of the little plot to do what she liked with. Hannah used to say 'I'd know which each of them gardings belonged to, ef I see 'em in Chiny'; and so she might, for the girls' tastes differed as much as their characters. Meg's had roses and heliotrope, myrtle, and a little orange tree in it. Jo's bed was never alike two seasons, for she was always trying experiments; this year it was to be a plantation of sunflowers, the seeds of which cheerful and aspiring plant were to feed 'Aunt Cockletop' and her family of chicks. Beth had old-fashioned, fragrant flowers in her garden — sweet peas, and mignonette, larkspur, pinks, pansies, and southernwood, with chickweed for the bird, and catnip for the pussies. Amy had a bower in hers — rather small and earwiggy, but very pretty to look at — with honeysuckles and morning-glories hanging their coloured horns and bells in graceful wreaths all over it; tall white lilies, delicate ferns, and as many brilliant, picturesque plants as would consent to blossom there.

LOUISA MAY ALCOTT *Little Women*
1869

LET'S MAKE A GARDEN

Some fine spring morning you're sure to have this idea. Then the first step is to get possession, by fair means or foul, of a piece of ground, which may or may not be possible. If it's not possible, that's certainly that. But it may be just half possible, which is really worse than being quite impossible. Parents and such-like will probably offer you that nice shady corner under the big tree where, as Father knows to his cost, absolutely nothing will grow. Maybe, of course, they are right. Father may know, also to his cost, that you'll have forgotten all about the seeds long before they begin to come up — in which case it doesn't much matter whether they come up or not. So, if you can't convince yourself that you will be as interested in that garden six months hence as you are this fine spring morning, don't take up gardening. But if you are convinced, then refuse, gently but firmly, to be fobbed off with the shady corner.

J R Evans *The Junior Week-end Book*
1939

ACKNOWLEDGEMENTS

We gratefully acknowledge permission to reprint extracts of copyright material in this book from the following authors, publishers and executors:

Angus & Robertson (Australia) *Cheerio Frank, Cheerio Everybody* by Frank Henning (1976)

Graham Binns for his letter to *The Times*

Robert Bly for the translation of *The Earthworm* by Harry Edmund Martinson from *Friends You Drank the Darkness* © Robert Bly

Jonathan Cape Ltd and the Estate of the Author for *Birches* from *The Poetry of Robert Frost* ed Edward Connery Latham

Curtis Brown *The Garden* (1946) and *In Your Garden Again* (1951) by Vita Sackville-West, copyright © Vita Sackville-West. Reproduced by permission of Curtis Brown London. *Those Were the Days* by AA Milne, copyright © AA Milne (published by Eyre Methuen 1929). Reproduced by permission of Curtis Brown London

Rupert Hart Davis (HarperCollins Publishers Ltd) for *My Family and Other Animals* by Gerald Durrell

Faber & Faber for *Autumn Journal* from *The Collected Poems of Louis MacNeice 1939*; *Cut Grass* and *The Trees* from *High Windows* by Philip Larkin

Cyril Fletcher for *Cyril Fletcher's Rose Book* and *Nice One Cyril*

Eric Glass Ltd (representatives of the **Beverley Nichols estate**) for *Garden Open Today* by Beverley Nichols and *The Gift of a Home* by Beverley Nichols

Hortus magazine for *Take Me to Your Hostas* (Spring 1989) by Nigel Colborn

Hutchinson (Publisher) and the Estate of the Author for *Green Fly* from *Green Fingers, A Present for Good Gardeners* by Reginald Arkell (Herbert Jenkins 1934)

Methuen for *Class* by Jilly Cooper

The Provost and Scholars of King's College Cambridge for *A Room with a View* by EM Forster

Little, Brown and Company (UK) Ltd for *Mrs Dale at Home* by Jonquil Antony (MacDonald and Co 1952)

Macmillan London Ltd *George – Don't Do That* by Joyce Grenfell (1977); *Maude Can't Come into the Garden*; *A Morbid Taste for Bones* by Ellis Peters (1977); *The Country Scene* by John Masefield

Macmillan Publishing Co Inc (NY) *The Royal Gardeners* by WE Shewell-Cooper (Cassell 1952)

Mr Frank Magro (copyright owner), and David Higham Associates Ltd for Osbert Sitwell, introduction to *The Making of Gardens* by Sir George Sitwell (Dropmore Press 1949 edition)

John Murray (Publishers) Ltd for *Harvest Hymn* from *John Betjeman – Collected Poems* ed Lord Birkenhead (1972)

Ann O'Connor for *Rhubarb Ted*

Penguin Books
A Love of Flowers by HE Bates (published by Michael Joseph Ltd 1971)
The Go-Between by LP Hartley (published by Hamish Hamilton 1953). Copyright © LP Hartley 1953. Reproduced by permission of Hamish Hamilton
Apples by Laurie Lee
Under the Autumn Garden by Jan Mark (Copyright © Jan Mark, 1977. Published by Kestrel Books)

The Pursuit of Love by Nancy Mitford (Penguin Books in association with Hamish Hamilton). Reprinted by permission of the Peters, Fraser and Dunlop Group Ltd

Punch Library for *Why Dogs Bite Gardeners* by Basil Boothroyd; *Parasite's Paradise* by Justin Richardson

Robson Books *The Bona Book of Julian and Sandy* by Barry Took and Marty Feldman 1978

The Literary Trustees of Walter de la Mare and The Society of Authors as their representative for *The Sunken Garden* by Walter de la Mare

The Times *Fourth Leaders from The Times* (1959). Copyright © Times Newspapers Ltd

Weidenfeld and Nicolson *The Parting Years 1963–74* by Cecil Beaton (1978);
Vita and Harold: The Letters of Harold Nicolson and Vita Sackville-West 1910–1962 ed Nigel Nicolson

Every effort has been made to contact copyright holders. We apologize for any unintentional errors or omissions.